# LAUGHTER and TEARS

# Laughter and Tears

## THOUGHTS ON FAITH
## IN FACE OF SUFFERING

*James A Whyte*

Series Editor: *Duncan B Forrester*

**SAINT ANDREW PRESS**
EDINBURGH

First published in 1993 by
SAINT ANDREW PRESS
121 George Street, Edinburgh EH2 4YN

Copyright © James A Whyte 1993

ISBN 0 7152 0682 6

**British Library Cataloguing in Publication Data**
A catalogue record for this book
is available from the British Library.

ISBN 0715206826

Cover photograph by *Paul Turner.*

Cover design by *Mark Blackadder.*

Printed and bound by Bell and Bain Ltd, Glasgow.

# Contents

# Editor's Introduction

ALL down the ages Christians have reflected on their faith and its bearing on life. These reflections have taken a great variety of forms, but one of the most common has been the sermon. For generations notable preachers were well-known public figures, and books of sermons were a well-known literary genre. In many places people queued to hear great preachers, whose sermons were reported in the press, and discussed and dissected afterwards. Sermons launched great movements of mission, and revival, and social change. Sometimes influential preachers were imprisoned by the authorities so that their disturbing challenge should not be heard.

Nowhere was this tradition more lively than in Scotland. But today, some people say, the glory has departed. If you want to find great preaching today, the critics say, go to Africa, or Latin America, or to Black churches in the States. No longer in Scotland do people pack in their hundreds into huge churches to hear great preachers. The sermon seems to have lost its centrality in Scottish life. The conviction and the emotional surcharge that once sustained a great succession of notable preachers seems hard to find today. Has secularisation destroyed the appetite for sermons? Has the modern questioning of authority eroded the preaching office? Do Christians no longer reflect on their faith, or do they do it in other and newer ways?

This series of books shows that the tradition of preaching is still very much alive and well. It has changed, it is true, and it has adapted to new circumstances and new challenges. It is not the same as it was in the long afterglow of the Victorian pulpit. Reflection by the Scots on their faith, as these books illustrate, is perhaps more varied than it was in the past, and their sermons are briefer. But Scottish preaching is still passionate, thoughtful, biblical, challenging, and deeply concerned with the relevance of the gospel to the needs of today's world.

The reflections on the Christian faith in these books are challenging, disturbing, nourishing. They proclaim a Word that is alive and active, and penetrates to the depths of things, a Word that speaks of hope and worth, of forgiveness and new beginnings, of justice, peace and love. And so they invite the reader to engage afresh with the everlasting gospel.

*Duncan B Forrester*

# Acknowledgments

I should like to express my warm thanks to Duncan Forrester for the help and encouragement he has given me in the preparation of this manuscript.

Above all, my thanks are due to Bill Henney and the people of Hope Park Church, St Andrews, for whom these sermons (all save the last) were originally written. They have shared my laughter and my tears, and I offer this book to them with affection and gratitude.

*James A Whyte*
ST ANDREWS

# 1

# Laughter and Tears

*Readings:* Isaiah 25:1-9; Matthew 7:1-12

*Text:* Revelation 21:3-4

> *Behold, the dwelling of God is with men. He will dwell with them*
> *and they shall be his people, and God himself will be with them;*
> *he will wipe away every tear from their eyes, and death shall be*
> *no more, neither shall there be mourning nor crying nor pain*
> *any more, for the former things have passed away.*

I want to ask a question—because it's one which keeps puzzling
me. Is the last word in life laughter, or is it tears?

Is it comedy or is it tragedy which comes nearest to the heart,
the truth, of human existence?

I was brought up to think that it was tragedy; I was taught at
school, for instance, that Shakespeare's tragedies are greater plays
than his comedies. Only now am I beginning to doubt that.

I wonder also if the real tragedies are not those of the great—
the Lears, the Macbeths, the Othellos—whose problems are largely
of their own making—but those of the poor and the weak. There
sticks in my mind from a newspaper report of one such tragedy the
image of a small boy standing by a swollen burn, crying, crying,
crying after his friend who had been swept away. And that brought
back memories of another small boy, from this congregation,
swept out to sea on a freak wave on an Easter Saturday morning.

*Before the beginning of years*
*There came to the making of man*
*Time, with a gift of tears,*
*Grief, with a glass that ran.*

Is grief inseparable from our mortality? Does it all end with Lear crying 'Howl! Howl! Howl! Howl!'? Must the last word be spoken in tears?

The Bible says 'No'. A very clear and decisive 'No'.

The ancient promise of Isaiah—'He will swallow up death forever, and the Lord God will wipe away tears from all faces'— is taken up in Revelation. I give it you this time in the slightly crisper English of the Good News Bible:

*Now God's home is with mankind! He will live with them and*
*they shall be his people. God himself will be with them and*
*be their God. He will wipe away all tears from their eyes.*
*There will be no more death, no more grief, or crying or pain.*
*The old things have disappeared.*

Now in one sense the old things have not disappeared. Death and grief, crying and pain are still with us. We may not mock with easy comfort those who hearts still ache and ache and ache again.

Yet those of us who have known grief and crying and pain— and that is most of us, at some time or another—would testify that there is one who makes himself known even in our tears, who in the midst of these old things that have not yet disappeared, can bring us mornings of joy for our evenings of tearfulness, trust for our trembling and hope for our fears.

The last word does not lie with tears. The Bible is emphatic about that.

What then of laughter? Here I find the Bible less explicit and less helpful. I hope you won't misunderstand me if I say it's a wee bit disappointing. Most of the references to laughter in the Bible are to scornful laughter. 'He will laugh them to scorn.' We read once in the Gospels that Jesus wept, but there is no mention of him laughing. Now that could be because his tears were so unusual as to excite notice, and his laughter so frequent as to be unremarkable. Maybe. But it is odd.

We are told that Jesus' teaching was full of humour, and that he made jokes. One of these is in the passage which we read— which we know as the saying about the Mote and the Beam. 'Why do you see the speck that is in your brother's eye and don't notice the log that is in your own eye?' That doesn't seem to us terribly funny, and it's difficult to imagine Jesus' hearers rolling about with laughter or rushing to catch their friends, saying, 'Have you heard the one about the mote and the beam?—This'll kill you!'

Maybe such sayings, or the one about the camel and the eye of the needle, really were funny to the Jews, because the Jew thought that grotesque exaggeration was hilarious, and we don't. A sense of humour varies from culture to culture, from person to person. Recently someone was talking, kindly enough, about a friend we have in common, and he said, 'Of course, he doesn't have a sense of humour.' I thought, 'That's odd.' Because I thought the other man had a delightful, gentle, playful sense of humour. Perhaps he hadn't always laughed at the other's more robust jokes.

But perhaps many of us don't find humour in the Bible because we've been taught not to expect it. Religion is a serious business. Reverence and laughter are not supposed to go together. When I was young we were not supposed to laugh in church. It's different now, I'm glad to say. But I think that we have learned to read the Bible with such solemnity that its humour and vitality cannot reach us.

3

Such an attitude is found in the Bible itself. When the author of Ecclesiastes says, 'Sorrow is better than laughter', and avers that, 'The laughter of fools is like the crackling of thorns under a pot'—you suspect that he considers that all laughter is frivolous, and that the wise man is always serious and grave.

That is just the attitude at which Jesus poked fun when he found it in the Pharisees. They must have known surely that he was getting at them when he told the story of the Prodigal Son and the Elder Brother. The prodigal returns and the father, overjoyed, orders feasting and laughter. For where there is feasting, there is laughter.

The older son returns from work, hears the music and dancing, and stays outside and sulks. A great grown man, behaving like a silly spoiled child, and talking like one! 'I've worked all the time and you never gave me a party.' It's funny, isn't it, the way we can behave when we're asked to welcome back a forgiven sinner?

Jesus more than once presents God's invitation as an invitation to a feast, which the pompous, the self-righteous, the over-serious cannot accept. And that image of the feast runs through the Bible, as the image of victory, of joy, laughter, good-humour, the vision of the way things ought to be and will be.

So maybe there's more about laughter in the Bible than we usually see.

I read once of a man who helped himself in the fight against cancer by getting videos of Laurel and Hardy films and laughing till his sides were sore. And it seems to have worked. The *Readers' Digest* magazine has been telling us for years that laughter is the best medicine, and maybe it's true. For in laughter we relax, we're seeing things in perspective, they fall into place.

Of course, it is we ourselves who have to be put in our proper place. The trouble with the Pharisees was not that they took religion too seriously, but that they took *themselves* too seriously.

4

When someone laughs, there is really only one thing to laugh at —that is, yourself. Those who have not learned to laugh at themselves, who take themselves too seriously, laugh at others in a way that is cruel and contemptuous. Such laughter is destructive. Perhaps it's that that is like the crackling of thorns under a pot. But those who have first learned to laugh at themselves warm the whole world with their laughter.

Laughter is subversive. It pricks the balloon of our pomposity. There is something anarchic about humour. 'The man who laughs has no master.' People in power and authority are often afraid of laughter—more afraid of laughter than they are of violence, for violence is their own language, and that they can understand. But laughter undermines their authority. In countries where freedom has been extinguished by tyranny, the only way the free spirit can express itself is by laughter and by making jokes. The joke is the only form of defiance.

In the former Soviet Union the voice of dissent was often the satirical magazine *Krokodil*, and something of the same defiant humour was expressed by writers like the Czech Milan Kundera. And I suppose the typical Glasgow humour is the humour of the powerless, laughing at the things they cannot control. When the M8 was being built right through Glasgow, a stranger stopped someone in Sauchiehall Street and asked the way to Charing Cross. 'It's doon there,' said the wee man, pointing in the direction of the road-works, 'if ye hurry.'

Umberto Eco's novel, *The Name of the Rose,* was at one level a medieval whodunit, but it had many other levels. The aspect which spoke most strongly to me was the picture of the old blind librarian of the monastery Jorge, the religious fanatic who feared laughter more than anything else, because he knew that the whole fabric of the Church's authority might dissolve if people learned to laugh.

Perhaps the most healthy thing in the General Assembly of the Church of Scotland is the laughter that often passes through it like a wave. Perhaps all our politicians, ecclesiastics and theologians would be better servants of the people and of God if they could laugh at themselves a little more.

Does everything then dissolve in flippancy and cynicism? No, for one thing more must be said. Only the one who suffers has a right to laugh. The man fighting cancer and the citizen of Prague or Moscow under Communism had this in common. Laughter is not our escape from tears and from suffering. The laughter of God is on the other side of our pain, the other side of our tears. Laughter is not carelessness, but the deepest kind of caring. Such laughter is the foretaste of heaven.

I remember very vividly the funeral of a dear friend, a much-loved minister who had been 'bishop' to a great succession of assistants. Tears there were, for there was a widow and a family and a congregation suddenly bereaved. There was a service that sustained our faith, and then, after the interment, we met in the church hall for a cup of tea, before all those who had travelled had to take their departure. It was a happy meeting of friends and acquaintances, who had this one thing in common—that they all loved this man. And we were sharing memories, telling stories of days gone by, and the hall was filled with talk and with loving laughter. I had a strong sense then that he was enjoying it too, and that already we were sharing with him in the laughter of heaven.

# 2

# The Military Metaphor
# in Religion

*Readings:* Joshua 1:1-9; Ephesians 6:10-20

*Text:* Ephesians 6:13

> *Therefore take the whole armour of God, that you may be able to withstand in the evil day, and having done all, to stand.*

The Lessons for this sermon came from the Lectionary. It seemed the only way in which I would ever come to a decision about what to preach this time. Too many different things have been going around in my mind.

Having decided to accept this discipline of the Lectionary, I found myself immediately arguing with the Lessons, because I have to admit that I'm not very fond of military metaphors in religion.

The story of Joshua is the story of a military commander who led the Israelites in a war of aggression, the invasion of a fertile country that was peacefully inhabited by other nations. Much could be made of the lovely call to courage, and the promise of God's presence, but the fact remains that what is described is a war of naked aggression. I could say more about that, but I won't.

In our passage from Ephesians, the writer uses warfare as the picture of the Christian life—a warfare against the spiritual forces of evil in the world, and he uses the familiar figure of the heavily armed Roman infantryman to describe the spiritual armour of the

Christian. It is a fine passage. Many great sermons have been preached on it. Some stirring hymns have been written about the Christian warfare with evil. But I'm still uncomfortable about the military metaphor.

I'm not a pacifist, so that's not my problem. I believe that sometimes a nation may be justified in taking up arms to counter aggression and injustice. But along with most soldiers and military people (and unlike some politicians) I believe that war must be the very last resort.

I happen also to believe that the religious war, the holy war, is always the most beastly and unbridled of all. Wars should be fought for limited ends, so that you know when you have won it and when it's time to stop, or you know when the game is no longer worth the candle. When war is fought for unlimited ends —for the cause of Christ against Satan, for example, or for the purity of Islam against all unbelievers—then there is no limit to its brutality, its cruelty, its horror. Crusades are always the most grisly of wars. In the crusade all the good—so you believe—is on your side and all the evil on the enemy's side. They cease to be human beings like yourselves.

We would all like to believe that the world is divided up into goodies and baddies, as it is in the old Western films that Ronald Reagan used to act in. But the world isn't like that, and it is very dangerous when politicians think it is.

I remember hearing recently the voice of George Bush on the radio. He was talking about the American decision to give China 'most-favoured nation' status. And this is what he said: 'It may be argued that a nation as moral and just as ours should not taint itself by associating with a nation less moral and less just.'

What does President Bush mean by a 'nation as moral and just as ours'? This is the man who was once the head of the CIA —how can *he* have such fantasies of self-righteousness?

Whenever world leaders start justifying themselves on high moral grounds, you know they're up to no good. And when they start seeing themselves as totally moral and the other side as utterly evil, you start building an air-raid shelter.

This tendency to see everything in black and white, to adopt a war-like stance, to look on those who disagree with you as enemies to be exterminated, is very common in human life.

Any of us who have tried to give help when a marriage is breaking down will know how one partner will come to you and tell a story that is quite horrifying about the way the other has behaved. But when you meet the other, you hear a totally different story. There is little hope for reconciliation until each comes to see that there is another side to the story and that not all the evil, not all the fault, is on the other side.

Paranoia is the name given to a mental illness whereby a person projects all the blame for his problems on to other people, and feels himself to be surrounded by enemies who are conspiring against him. In a fully developed form this can produce very dangerous fantasies. But in a very mild form it possibly exists in most of us. When things are going badly we get paranoid, rather than admit that we have failed. In the kind of marriage situation I've described above, or in quarrels within the Church, which in the past I've had to deal with, if you suggest to your friend, however mildly, that the faults are not all on the one side, you have gone over to the enemy, and you have lost a friend.

So I'm chary of the military metaphor, because I don't want to encourage paranoid politics or paranoid religion—I think we have too much of both already. Paranoid politics identifies the other party as the enemy, to be destroyed by any means, fair or foul. So instead of genuine thought and the sharing of concern, you get the shouting of slogans, the massaging of figures, and downright dishonesty in order never to admit mistakes, and, of course, to win the next election. I sometimes think that democracy would be much better served if we could get rid of the party system altogether.

The same can be said about paranoid religion. Paranoid Protestantism may see Roman Catholicism as the enemy. Paranoid Fundamentalism in the United States used to see Communism as the enemy, and they're in trouble at the moment because they've lost an enemy and have no one to fight against.

I suppose Paranoid Catholicism sees Protestantism as the enemy of the true faith and looks forward to the day when the Catholic Church will be the only Church, having won back the position and the power it had in the middle ages.

But wait a minute. Are there no real enemies, no real evils in the world? Are there not some things to which we have to say a firm resounding 'No'? Are there not some people who are really dangerous? As someone once wrote on a wall, 'Just because you're paranoid, it doesn't mean they're *not* out to get you.'

Surely there are evils that must be resisted, and a spiritual warfare against them. Indeed there are. The great problem is to identify them. There is a story of the young MP being taken into the House of Commons by a senior member of his own party. As they sat down, the young man looked at the benches opposite and said, 'It's great to be face to face with the enemy.' To which the old man replied, 'Na, na laddie. That is the Opposition. Your enemies are all on this side.'

If you think all evil is on the other side, you don't see the evil in yourself or in your Church or in your party. James Hogg, the Ettrick Shepherd, wrote a wonderful book called *The Private Memoirs and Confessions of a Justified Sinner*, in which a young man becomes so obsessed with the need to exterminate evil that he becomes the agent of the devil, the mysterious, and very orthodox, friend who is always at his elbow. Hogg's book is a satire on a certain kind of Calvinism, but it applies to more than that, and it reminds one of Jesus' satires on the self-righteous, who strain at gnats, and swallow camels.

Does our New Testament passage help us?

Well, the Christian warfare, according to the writer to the Ephesians, is not with flesh and blood. That is, the enemy, for the Christian is not other people. So if for you the enemy are 'Catholics' or 'Protestants', or 'Communists' or 'Pro-lifers' or 'Anti-lifers' (and how misleading all these labels are) your warfare is not the Christian warfare. Human beings are not to be seen as the enemy—our warfare is against spiritual forces. If it is evil we are against, we must not see any human being, however wicked, however misguided, as simply the embodiment of evil. When we do that, we may be sure the evil has got into ourselves. The conviction that the devil is over there stops us realising that he is at our elbow.

But what I find cheering in this passage is the number of times the word 'stand' is used. The armour of God is offered to us not for aggression, but for defence, for our protection in an evil world. Truth, justice, peace, faith, salvation, God's word of Love—these we put on so that we may stand firm when under attack.

I don't know if I'm a peaceable person. I'm certainly a lazy person. I don't willingly get into a fight. I like a quiet life. I don't go about looking for causes to get steamed up about. Maybe that is my weakness of character—though I wouldn't like to be the kind of person who has to have a cause to do battle for. But when I do get into a fight, it is usually because there is some point at which I have to take a stand against something which seems to me to be wrong. Sometimes, in addition, because I cannot let down a friend.

Now the fights I am talking about are not fought with fists —I gave up that kind of thing when I left the school playground.

11

They are fought with words, sometimes in print, but usually in the Presbytery and the General Assembly—although there were one or two also in the Faculty of Divinity and the Senatus of the University. You'll have your places.

For me there are three points of testing, particularly. The first is when you are tempted to sit down and say nothing when you know you ought to stand up and be counted. The fact that a lot of other people are doing the same thing and sitting on their hands is no excuse. That is the temptation of cowardice, and I am often guilty of that. The second point of testing is when you are engaged in the struggle, and you are tempted to twist the argument a bit, to be not too careful about the truth. That is the temptation of un-scrupulousness. And the third point of testing is, if and when you have won your fight, to exult in victory. 'We smote them hip and thigh, we had them on the run.' That is the temptation of pride, of arrogance.

Now you see these evils are not out there in someone else, they are right here in me. It is against these I have to be armed with the armour of God if I am going to be his soldier, if the battles I fight are to be his battles. To do it his way requires courage, conscience and compassion. And the real enemies of these are not out there, but here in me—my cowardice, my corner-cutting, my conceit. It is against them that I need to be armed with the belt of truth, the breastplate of justice, the sandals of peace, the shield of faith, the helmet of salvation and the sword of the spirit.

So take the armour of God, and be careful how you identify the enemy.

# 3

# Robed in Dreadful Majesty

*Readings:* Isaiah 2:10-19; Revelation 1:4-16

*Text:* Isaiah 2:10

> *Enter into the rock, and hide in the dust, from before the terror of the Lord and from the glory of his majesty.*

This is the season of Advent, when the Church thinks about the judgment of God, Christ's coming in judgment. And what started me thinking was Charles Wesley's magnificent Advent Hymn, which I love singing—and then wonder why I should enjoy so much a hymn which is so fearsome. The Hymn is:

> *Lo! he comes with clouds descending,*
> *once for favoured sinners slain.*

Wesley took the first verse almost straight from the Book of Revelation, chapter 1, verse 7:

> *Behold, he is coming with the clouds,*
> *and every eye will see him,*
> *every one who pierced him;*
> *and all tribes of the earth*
> *will wail on account of him.*

The second verse of the Hymn begins:

*Every eye shall now behold him*
*Robed in dreadful majesty*

and Wesley may have had in mind there the description in the first chapter of Revelation, of:

*... one like a son of man, clothed with a long robe and with a golden girdle round his breast; his head and his hair were white as wool, white as snow, his feet were like burnished bronze, refined as in a furnace, and his voice was like the sound of many waters; in his right hand he held seven stars, from his mouth issued a sharp two-edged sword, and his face was like the sun shining in full strength.*

But, now, here is my problem. What is this? Is this the Jesus that we know from the Gospels? The carpenter of Nazareth, the encourager of little children, the healer of the woman with the issue of blood, the teacher of love, the one who brought forgiveness—to the paralysed man, to the woman taken in adultery, to the woman at the well, to the soldiers who killed him. Can it be the same Jesus who comes 'robed in dreadful majesty'? Can it be the same Jesus coming not to forgive, but to judge?

The expectation that the end of the world was coming, and that Jesus would appear again in glory, to judge both the living and the dead, was one of the beliefs of the early Christians. They believed that it would happen in their lifetime. But the end of the world didn't come, and as generation after generation came and went, Christians tended to replace the expectation of the end of the world, with the hope of going to heaven when you die.

But the idea of a day of judgment lingered on, and some

Christians in every generation have searched the writings of the Old and New Testament for the signs that would tell them when it is going to happen, and some will give you a very plausible account of exactly in what order things are going to happen. When we came to the year AD 1000, many people thought that the end would come then, and doubtless many will have the same idea as we approach the year 2000. I have no doubt that the only text worth paying any attention to in that matter is the one that says, 'No one knows the day or the hour.'

Much more important than the question 'when?' is the question 'what?'—*what* is it that we ought to expect, hope for, or, perhaps, fear?

In the Middle Ages the operative word was 'fear.' The theme of the Last Judgment was popular with Medieval artists, who excelled themselves in depicting the anguish of the damned as they were taken away down to hell. Sometimes, as in the Cathedral in Torcello, near Venice, the west wall would have a mosaic—or fresco or stained-glass window—depicting the Last Judgment, so that the congregation saw this as they were going out of church. And such was the effect of this constant portrayal of Jesus as the Judge, 'robed in dreadful majesty', that men and women turned not to Jesus but to his mother for tenderness and understanding, forgiveness and love. The cult of the virgin flourished because Jesus was depicted as majestic judge rather than as companion and friend.

So what has happened? It seems as though Christians, having believed that at his first coming Jesus made God known through the poverty of the stable, in the dust of the Galilean road, by the love that was freely available to the sinners and the poor, the timid and the humble, and by the self-giving of the Cross, then came to believe that at his second coming God will be made known through power and might, judgment and terror. It is as though they imagine him at his second coming clothed in all the things that he rejected during his life on earth—the pomp and the privilege and the power of an earthly king, multiplied by infinity. 'Robed in dreadful majesty.'

Should we then abandon all idea of judgment? That is what we are tempted to do. A friend of mine told me how, in his first ministry, a congregation member kept asking him to preach about the second coming. He had never given much thought to the this, and wasn't too anxious to begin, but she kept pestering him. One day, while visiting a wise old woman of his flock, he confided to her his problem. She answered, 'Ech, laddie, there's a wheen fowk mak a gey steer about the second comin' wha haena dune muckle aboot the first yin yet.' My friend felt a lot better.

Yet that story itself suggests to me that we do need to keep the idea of judgment, but to remember who it is that is our judge. The question for judgment is, 'Have we taken the first coming seriously?'

'He that judges me is the Lord,' says Paul. For me that means the same Jesus who walked the roads of Galilee and the streets of Jerusalem, whom we name Saviour, Redeemer. He does not change character. What he reveals to us is the character of the Eternal God.

Therefore the last, the ultimate judgment on us and on our world is the judgment of love. 'Robed in dreadful majesty'? Yes, indeed. Robed in the dreadful majesty of love.

Perhaps preachers like me, who want to encourage the fearful and to comfort the desolate through the gospel of God's grace, God's acceptance, God's love, fail sometimes to tell ourselves and others that the obverse side of the coin of love is a sternness, a persistent demand that we would rather forget than face.

Love can be terrible in its demands and frightening in its consequences.

Love will not leave us in the dust or in the mire. Love demands that we be the best that we can be. Love's demand is that we also be loving. What is the object and aim of God's persistent love, save that we also become loving, and so share in his loving?

I often come back to the First Letter of John and the fourth chapter where he makes that deceptively simple statement, 'God is love,' and adds, 'and he who abides in love abides in God and God in him.' But he also says, 'He who does not love does not know God; for God is love.' So there is an exclusive side to the comforting saying, 'God is love.' It is not only grace, it is also judgment. The unloving know nothing of God.

The demand that we be loving is an unending demand, it is open-ended, it is a blank cheque. We would like to set limits to it. To say, 'Lord, of course I will love my family, and always do my best for them, but let me leave my loving there.' Or, 'I will stand by my friends, through thick and thin, but don't ask me to love my enemies.' But that is precisely what he does ask, and to the question 'Who is my neighbour?', he answers with a story that forces us to see that our neighbour is anyone who is in need.

Of course, we have to set limits to our loving for the simple reason that we are human beings, and not God, that we have limited resources, and can be only in one place at one time. So we can't answer every appeal that comes through the letter-box, and we can't respond to every demand on our time, to do things that other people could do and neglect the things that only we can do. That is a problem particularly in the ministry. We're not omnipotent, we can't be responsible for everything, and we need to accept that quite cheerfully and with a good conscience. But that is not really to set a limit to our loving, that is to direct it wisely.

For the demand of love is always there, and it is always stretching us beyond where we want to go. God, someone has suggested, is easy to please, but hard to satisfy. And it can be frightening in its consequences. We don't know where the road will end. We cheerfully take the vows of marriage—for better, for worse, for richer, for poorer, in sickness and in health—without reflecting what these words may mean in sheer devotion, visiting in hospital, week after week after week, the one who once could smile and joke and fill one's days with joy, and now no more.

In the same way, those who commit themselves to people and to justice and to truth never know where that loyalty may take them.

What they do discover, those who are prepared to venture in love, and to take the consequences, is that they may be cast down, but they are not destroyed; hard-pressed, but not forsaken. 'Whoever abides in love, abides in God.'

And what we believe is that love not only stands before us, to search us to the core, and judge us—it is love that stands in terrible majesty to judge the world: to judge the world's love-lessness, its cruelty, its injustice, its greed. The ultimate judgment, the judgment before which a harsh, acquisitive world should indeed quail, and must indeed quail, is the judgment of love. The wrath of God, the anger of God, as George Macdonald said, is his love seen from the other side.

Covetousness in the New Testament is called idolatry. Yet some people speak today as if it were the most creative of virtues. Top executives now feel hard done by if they're not getting six-figure salaries, and a 25 per cent increase each year. Was it last year I read of a woman who at Christmas spent £43,000 on a number plate for her daughter's BMW? What would Amos or Isaiah have said about that?

*Their land is filled with silver and gold, and there is no end to their treasures .... Their land is filled with idols: they bow down to the work of their hands .... Enter into the rock and hide in the dust from before the terror of the Lord and from the glory of his majesty. The haughty looks of man shall be brought low, and the pride of men shall be humbled: and the Lord alone shall be exalted in that day.*

*And men shall enter the caves of the rocks and the holes of the ground, from before the terror of the Lord, and from the glory of his majesty, when he rises to terrify the earth.*

This is the indignation of love against the lovelessness of men, and love's indignation is indeed terrible to behold, and robed in dreadful majesty.

# 4

# Waking the
# Sleeping Beauty

*Readings:* Genesis 1:1-8; 2 Corinthians 4:1-6; Matthew 5:14-16

*Text:* Matthew 5:16

> *Let your light so shine before men that they may see your good works and glorify your Father which is in heaven.*

The first Sunday in February was traditionally called 'Candlemas.' As the name suggests, candles were distributed that Sunday, and when each worshipper held a lighted candle, the dark medieval church would be a blaze of light.

In these dark northern parts Candlemas would celebrate the strengthening of the light after the darkest days of winter were over. But, more importantly, it celebrated the gift of Jesus Christ to be the light of the world, the light that is never darkened, no matter how gloomy and severe our winters. They would remember Simeon in the Temple, holding the infant Jesus in his arms and calling him, 'A light to lighten the Gentiles.' They might remember John's words about God's light in Christ—'The light shines in the darkness and the darkness has never mastered it.'

This then is Candlemas. 'How far that little candle throws his beams,' says Portia in Shakespeare's *Merchant of Venice*. 'So shines a good deed in a naughty world.'

And Jesus said to his disciples, 'You are the light of the world

.... Let your light so shine before men that they may see your good deeds and glorify your Father in heaven.'

Jesus here seems to be suggesting that we should hug the limelight, that we should seek publicity. Yet elsewhere he pours scorn on the Pharisees who were always parading their goodness before men, and he urged his disciples not to be like that. When you pray, go into your room where only God will see you. When you give alms, don't let your left hand know what your right hand is up to. Keep it under wraps.

Yet here he seems to be saying, 'Do it all out in front. Sound the trumpet. Let the light shine.'

Now I confess, and maybe you would too, that I'm more impressed by the modest than by the flamboyant. Most of the good work the Church does gets no publicity and little praise. Whereas those who sing their own praises arouse our suspicion. I have long been suspicious of the publicity-seekers—of the trumpeted evangels, the great campaigns and crusades which promise to change the Church and the world. They always claim great success, but when the tumult and the shouting die, nothing much has changed.

What does Jesus mean then when he says 'You are the light of the world' and 'Let your light shine'?

He uses two thumbnail sketches to illustrate what he means. First, a city set on a hill cannot be hid. Second, no one lights a lamp and then covers it up to stop anyone seeing it—they put it on a stand so that it can give light to the whole house. The two pictures, of the city on the hill, and the lamp on the candlestick, are essentially the same. There's no hiding them, that's the point. It's foolish to try.

There is something fundamental about the thought of light— as if deep in the universe and in our hearts there is a conflict and a choice between light and darkness. The creation story in Genesis begins with chaos and darkness, but the darkness is scattered, order emerges, when God says, 'Let there be light.' Light—God's first gift to the world.

Light shines without effort. You can't stop it shining. Some of us can remember the black-out in the Second World War, and how extraordinarily difficult it was to black-out your windows so that chinks of light wouldn't get out and be seen by German bombers.

Let the light shine, said Jesus. You don't have to black it out, that's all. Just let it shine and people will see it.

Let your light shine before men. But what is this light? Again, we come back to the Pharisee. He let his light shine all right. He paraded his good works. Does Jesus want us to be a lot of little Jack Horners, enjoying life's good things and saying, 'What a good boy am I'?

It is, alas, too easy for Christians and congregations to do just that. To say to the world, 'Look how good we are. We are all pious, decent respectable folk here. No drug-addicts, alcoholics or drop-outs or criminals here. We don't have anything to do with people like that.' And then we have become the Pharisee, who was so happy reciting his good works before God that he could only spare a glance at the sad, broken man at the other end of the pew, and then only to despise him. But it was the sad, broken man that God was paying attention to.

What the Pharisee in us forgets, again and again, is the source of the light. Light is God's gift—his first gift—to the world.

Paul writing to the Christians at Corinth remembers the text in Genesis, and says, 'It is the God who said, "Let light shine out of darkness", who has shone in our hearts to give the light of the knowledge of the glory of God in the face of Jesus Christ.'

Many religions and many theologians have thought they knew where the glory of God was to be found and seen—in the wonders of nature, in the magnificence of great temples and churches, in the pomp and ceremony of great processions and services. Christianity alone can say that his glory is perfectly seen in a human face—not in the face of king or a pope or a great one, but in the face of the carpenter of Nazareth.

God's perfect glory is to be seen in the face of perfect love.

And that is the light we have to allow to shine. We are not the source. We are the reflectors.

What makes a living, shining Church? Is it the number of organisations that we have, the enthusiasm of office-bearers, the commitment of members? No one is going to doubt the importance of these things, as signs of life: but they are not the *source* of life. And there is a tendency, when the Church is not being noticeably successful, for us to think that it can be organised into life. And we keep appointing organisers to do this for us—organisers of evangelism and of other things. It seems that the smaller the Church becomes, the more organisers it appoints. They are well-meaning people most of them, anxious to do a good job, and they sit in their offices devising programmes, and they come down to Presbyteries and congregations to chivvy us into enthusiasm for their programmes. But good church people, already overburdened, find it hard to keep up with all of this, or to find others to do it, and they get more and more discouraged, and so do the organisers. And we all feel a little more guilty than we felt before.

I have on my shelves a little book about the renewal of the Church, with the intriguing title, *Shaking the Sleeping Beauty*. On the front cover is a picture of the Sleeping Beauty, slumbering until the coming of her prince. And the book pictures the Church as the sleeping beauty, which has to be awakened to her mission. The author wanted, as the blurb says, to arouse the Church from its slumbers and challenge it to wake up to its mission.

Now, in my time lots of people have tried to shake me awake.

I've been scolded, I've been hectored, I've been chivvied by preachers, speakers, orators, in the Church and out of it, at Presbytery meetings and at political meetings, to do the things they think must be done if the Church is to come alive or the world is to be put to rights. And I have to confess—and if you detect a note of cynicism in this, you may not be wrong—that the longer I live the more counter-suggestible I become. The more people shake me by the shoulder and tell me to march for Jesus, or whatever the latest thing is, the more I want to stay at home—and I usually do.

But this is not just cynicism—because I perceive, and I think others see this too, that many of these special efforts, and attempts to shake us into some kind of activity—any kind of activity, I sometimes think—are not the overflow of faith and hope and love, but rather the outflow of doubt, desperation and frustration, disguised in frenzied activity or angry denunciation.

Such things can never shake the Church into life.

Yet I like the picture of the Church as a Sleeping Beauty. For there are great resources in the Church. Within people who think of themselves as very ordinary people, there are great resources of faith and loving waiting to be awakened, waiting to be set free.

But how are they to be set free? Isn't there something odd about the title of my little book, *Shaking the Sleeping Beauty*?

Do you remember the fairy-story of the Sleeping Beauty? How was she to be awakened? No amount of shaking or shouting in her ear was ever going to waken the Sleeping Beauty. There was only one thing that could bring her back into light and life, and that was the kiss of love.

There, in the fairy-story, is a gospel insight we often forget. No amount of shaking, or shouted exhortations from pulpit or platform, hectoring sermons or passionate speeches, is going to waken the Church to be the shining light that it can become. The

24

only thing that can waken the Church is the kiss of love. We cannot be scolded into life, we can only be *loved* into life.

We can only be loved into life. And the Christian gospel is that God does love us into life. It is that kiss of God's love and his forgiveness, telling us that in spite of our failures we are worthwhile; and in spite of our foolishness, he trusts us: that alone wakens us to the light, and brings liberty and love to life within us.

And then the light shines. For people who have learned what it is to be loved by God, find that the same love and sympathy, compassion and concern flow out to others. They don't need to be shaken or pushed. The eye of their imagination is opened and they do things because they come from their hearts. And then their good works are seen.

It seems to me that that is happening where people hear the good news of God's love for us, waken from the sleep of a purely conventional religion, and begin to do things, not because they have been scolded or exhorted or pushed, but because God's love has wakened them into loving action for his Church and for his needy world.

But remember that it's the light of God's love that we see in the face of Jesus Christ, and it's his light that, please God, by some miracle of his grace, some may see reflected in our faces. His is the light, and his the glory.

# 5

# The Service of the Mystery

COMMISSIONING OF INDUSTRIAL CHAPLAINS
ABERDEEN: ST NICHOLAS (4 SEPTEMBER 1991)

*Readings:* Job 28; Matthew 6:19-34

*Text:* Ephesians 3:9 (Authorised Version)

> *... and to make all men see what is the fellowship of the mystery which from the beginning hath been hid in God who created all things by Jesus Christ ...*

In this impressive service we have commissioned Industrial Chaplains for work in the North East and in the offshore oil industry, and we have paid tribute to the work already accomplished. The task of a preacher is to see what light God's word sheds on what we have been doing this evening, and on the work of Industrial Chaplaincy.

But there is an immediate problem for the preacher. The world of modern technology and the world of the Bible are very far apart. Much of the industry in the North East now is related to the oil industry. There is clearly nothing in the Bible about the technical, economic, human or ecological problems of oil exploration and exploitation.

There is, however, a very remarkable poem set into the Book of Job, which describes with admiration the ingenuity and the daring of men who mine for silver and gold and precious stones:

*Surely there is a mine for silver, and a place for gold which they
      refine.*
*Man puts is hand to the flinty rock, and overturns mountains
      by the roots.*
*He cuts out channels in the rocks, and his eye sees every
      precious thing.*
*He binds up the streams that they do not trickle, and the thing
      that is hid he brings forth to light.*

'The thing that is hid he brings forth to light.' That is what
has been happening and is happening around here. The resources
of oil and gas, hidden for long ages beneath the ocean bed, are
brought to light through man's daring and ingenuity. That can be
said not only of oil and gas, but of modern industry and technology in general—it is bringing hidden things to light. I was able to
write this sermon on a word-processor, because the resourceful-
ness of humanity has brought to light the hidden possibilities of
the silicon chip.

This beautiful poem in Job celebrates the cleverness of the
mining technology of his time, and the courage of those who
work in such dangerous places. If he can admire, how much more
can we. Even considering that, by the standards of next century
our present oil platforms will be regarded as very primitive
structures, one can only wonder at the human intelligence and
the fearlessness of those who in our day seek the things that are
hid, and bring them forth to light.

But immediately the poet brings us up short. 'But where shall
wisdom be found? And where is the place of understanding?'
Can we find wisdom by digging deep into the earth or boring
beneath the ocean bed, or exploring the intricacies of the silicon
chip? All these precious and valuable things, gold, silver,
precious stones, iron, copper, oil and gas and silicon are not to

be compared in value with the wisdom that understands what are the things that really matter, that knows what it's all in aid of, that has a glimpse of the purposes of God.

But then the author ends this magnificent poem with what seems to be a trite and banal statement of orthodox piety: 'Behold, the fear of the Lord, that is wisdom; and to depart from evil is understanding.' It's like many a children's sermon. He has told a lovely story only to end by saying, 'Now, be good, boys and girls.'

But the poet in Job is not really like the patronising preachers of children's sermons. He is a sceptic. His conclusion is that it is not given to man to find the hidden wisdom of God, or to understand his purposes. All that we can do is to be reverent before the mystery and obey the commandments.

But perhaps even that is to see further than many do in our industrial and political life today. Asked what are the things that really matter, what's it in aid of, they would answer honestly— 'Money'. They are not trying to serve God and Mammon, they are quite simply and wholeheartedly serving Mammon, Money. Money is the name of the game. That appears to be the basic assumption in the modern world. And where that is the basic assumption, there is little interest in Industrial Chaplaincy or in anything other than the maximising of profit.

I remember a cartoon that appeared after one of our financial scandals, of the boss sitting behind a large desk, smoking a large cigar, and glaring at the terrified job-candidate opposite. The caption was, 'And we need someone who can distinguish between right and wrong—should the need ever occur.'

But there are more signs that people, managers and workers, are rediscovering that to have money as your only value is self-destructive; that the very functioning of our high-tech industries and our commerce and finance depends on there being other values besides money to guide, to propel and to restrain them.

The setting up of the chaplaincy to the Off-shore Oil Industry was itself one such sign, which should be an encouragement to others. It is the human face of industry, a recognition, as Andrew Wylie has said, that industry's greatest resource is people. And it is not only in time of disaster that those in industry find themselves awed before the mystery of things and needing to understand both good and evil. Mystery meets us in the everyday. Death and injury, pain and loss confront us all in human life, yet often it is in them we find courage and self-sacrifice, goodness and generosity and learn their value.

While I was thinking of these things, there kept coming into my head a phrase from Ephesians, '... and to make all men see what is the fellowship of the mystery, which from the beginning of the world hath been hid in God.' For these words—'the fellowship of the mystery'—express the relationship of minister and people in the parish, and of chaplain, full-time or part-time, and those at every level in industry.

'To make all men see what is the fellowship of the mystery.' It has to begin at the level of our common humanity, of sharing the experiences of everyday life before we share with them also those experiences when we touch the beyond in the midst of things, when we become aware of the things that matter more than money or clothing or food.

People are aware of this dimension of life far more than they are prepared to talk about it, but they will show often by the warmth of a greeting or the clasp of a hand that they have seen it. We reassure them, by representing to them the fellowship of the mystery, and by our caring, which itself is part of the mystery.

Now, I have to be honest and tell you that these words—'the fellowship of the mystery'—are a happy mistranslation in the Authorised Version. Modern versions say 'dispensation' or 'plan', because the Greek word is not the usual word for fellowship, but is our word 'economy.' The stress is not on our sharing with each other, but on the way God dishes it out. But that, after all, is precisely what people often want to talk about—the way God seems to have dished it out to them. And we need to share that with them.

But my text has started half-way through a sentence—one of those long sentences you get in Ephesians. Let me go back to the beginning:

> *To me, though I am the very least of all the saints, this grace was given, to preach to the Gentiles the unsearchable riches of Christ, and to make all men see what is the plan of the mystery, hidden for ages in God who created all things ....*

Perhaps Industrial Mission is the equivalent in our time of preaching to the Gentiles, to those who didn't seem to be within God's plan, many of whom didn't care whether they were or not. What is to be preached, what they need to find and see is a wealth that is unsearchable—that cannot be dug out of the hills, as the ancient miners dug out their precious metals and precious stones, nor tapped from the ocean bed, like the black, black oil—the unsearchable riches of Christ.

And this wealth is unsearchable in the sense that its boundaries cannot be traced, it cannot be enclosed in a slogan or a dogma, or in a nice turn of phrase from the preacher's vocabulary of theological terms. There is always more of it than we have yet discovered, more to it than we can understand. The mystery remains a mystery. But what for the poet in Job was a dark mystery of the incomprehensible ways of God with man, has become for the Christian the bright mystery of the unsearchable riches of Christ. For in him we can see a love that goes down into the darkness of death itself and is not conquered.

I'm told that it is hard to get ministers to undertake part-time industrial chaplaincies. And certainly with linkings and unions of parishes, ministers have less slack on the rope than they ever had before. Yet I wonder if they realise how they are impoverishing their ministry if they refuse. For surely it is the greatest privilege to be able to stand by men and women in their ordinary concerns of work and play, of money and clothing and food, representing always the mystery that is within and beyond these things—the mystery of life and of death, of love and of suffering. And then when they confront the mystery, and can evade it no longer, to be there in the fellowship of the mystery, to find the unsearchable riches of Christ, and be the reassurance that neither death, nor life, nor angels, nor principalities, nor things present, nor things to come, nor powers, nor height, nor depth, nor anything else in all creation, will be able to separate us from the love of God in Christ Jesus our Lord.

# 6

# Illusion and Reality

*Readings:* Psalm 73:12-28; Acts 8:9-24

I'm sure that if I mention Virtual Reality, everyone will know more about it than me. I did go so far as to buy Howard Rheingold's massive book about it. Virtual Reality, as I understand it, promises us the ultimate in simulators such as they use in the services for flying instruction and driving instruction. You sit alone in a room, and you wear earphones and goggles, and you experience a totally new world.

Of course, when we watch television we are experiencing a new world, but that experience is not total. Even when I am absorbed in the news, I am also aware of the arm of my chair and of my familiar room, and when the commercials come on I switch off the sound and go and make a cup of tea. With virtual reality, however, the experience seems to involve everything. So it has been called 'virtual reality', using the word 'virtual' in the sense of almost, as near as nothing. But is this artificial experience really so close to reality, or is it the biggest illusion of all? Is it possible, as Rheingold claims, to grasp reality through illusion?

It has never been easy for human beings to distinguish between what is real and what is illusion. The mirage is totally convincing. The full moon can look enormous as it rises over the horizon: but we know that it is in reality the same size as when it is high in the sky. Our very experience of the sun going round the earth is illusion, but it took mankind a long time, and considerable suffering, to come to accept that it is we who are moving, not the sun.

Our dreams, and our day dreams are illusions, I suppose, and we can enjoy these—as we can be enriched by novels and films and plays and television—so long as we know the difference between the dream and the reality. When we no longer know the difference, we're in trouble.

A hypnotist can put someone into a trance and make them see a toy dog as a dangerous lion, or a piece of string as a poisonous snake. That is illusion, and very powerful it can be. I suspect that many of the illusionists of the ancient world, like Simon the Magician in our New Testament lesson, were using a form of hypnotism to make things appear and disappear—and of course our stage and television magicians, like Paul Daniels, are adept at making us look at one thing while the sleight of hand is being performed elsewhere.

So what is illusion and what is real? Is religion illusion? That is what some people say. Religion is just wishful thinking, God is simply a projection of our unconscious, and we have all been mesmerised or hypnotised into believing that there's something there when there isn't.

So it has been said. Now, I wouldn't like to pretend that there is no element of illusion in religion. Religious people are often deluded, are often guilty of wishful thinking, often project their own needs and fears on to God. I think we have to recognise that, and to beware of it in ourselves, for religious delusions can be very powerful and very destructive.

But to say that all religion, all faith, is simply illusion, that's quite another thing.

That's usually said by people who pride themselves on being hard, matter-of-fact realists: no-nonsense people. Now I spend a lot of time arguing against what I think is nonsense in religion, because some people seem ready to believe any kind of nonsense nowadays. But my no-nonsense friends tend to think that the only things that are real are the things that you can see and touch and taste and buy and sell. Material things, and especially the money that enables you to have them. These are reality—anything else is illusion.

The Psalmist who wrote the 73rd Psalm was taken in for a bit by this view of real life. He confesses, 'I was envious of the arrogant, when I saw the prosperity of the wicked.' He saw the materialist prosper. He was thinking not perhaps so much of people who can pay themselves enormous salary increases, but rather of something more thuggish than that. It's the mafia type of person he has in mind, the one who makes himself rich by violence and oppression, who becomes so powerful that everyone flatters him, and most of them are in his pocket. And he is envious of people like that because they get off with it—they're not in trouble like other people. 'Behold, these are the wicked; always at ease, they increase in riches.' He envies them because they've got it made, and he who has kept his hands clean has had nothing but trouble.

Until, he says, I went into the sanctuary of God. Then in God's house he sees this reality in a quite different light. Where is reality and where is illusion? The wicked, with all their riches, are the illusion. Truly they are no more substantial than a dream. All these things will disappear, and they with them. 'Like a dream when a man rouses himself, O Lord, like images in sleep which are dismissed on waking.'

He becomes ashamed of his envy of the rich and wicked, because he realises that he, the poor and not very prosperous Psalmist, has riches that they know nothing of—he has the companionship of God:

*Nevertheless, I am continually with thee, thou dost hold my right hand.*

*Whom have I in heaven but thee, and there is nothing on earth that I desire besides thee.*

Wishful thinking? Or a deeper view of reality?

For another answer, let's turn to that other materialist, Simon Magus. He was a magician, an illusionist. How he did it, we don't know—but then I don't know how Paul Daniels does it either. Simon could make people see things that weren't there, and by his tricks had built up a great reputation for magic power, and had made a lot of money in the process.

Simon was not a pure materialist though, for when Philip came to Samaria and preached about Jesus, Simon with a lot of others, believed him, and was baptised. But what aroused his professional interest were the miracles—presumably of healing—that followed Philip's preaching. This magic, he was humble enough to recognise, was stronger than anything he could perform.

When Peter and John came down to Samaria, and more wonders began to happen, Simon was even more impressed, and he decided to take a post-graduate course in magic. He said, 'Will you show me how to do it, and I'll pay you the fees—I've got the money here.'

What he got from Peter was a very dusty reply. Peter was very good at dusty replies, delivered dramatically from a great height. 'Your money perish with you,' he said. I must say, I think Peter was a bit hard on Simon, who, given his background, had made an understandable mistake. Simon must have been a sincere man, for he took the rebuke very well. But Peter was right, of course. The Apostles were not magicians. This was not a technique that could be learned and mastered, like juggling or sleight of hand or hypnotism. The Holy Spirit comes only as a gift, and God only

35

is master of the gift. Here was a reality that Simon hadn't understood.

Mind you, perhaps Peter was so touchy because the truth is that every preacher, every evangelist, has techniques, has a craft, whether he or she is a run-of-the-mill performer in a small town pulpit, or a great evangelist drawing thousands to some stadium or other. We have ways of beginning and of ending—not always soon enough, I grant—we use humour, word-pictures, whatever, not just to keep you from falling asleep, but to communicate, if we can, some insight, some enthusiasm. There are tricks of the trade which we are all using, consciously or unconsciously, well or badly. In the case of the great evangelist they may be so powerful and hypnotic that people do things they never meant to do and say afterwards, 'I don't know what came over me.' Sometimes it is just magic, though sometimes it may be the Holy Spirit. But all of us, little preachers or great, are in danger sometimes of using the tricks to conceal the fact that we have nothing to say, that the Holy Spirit is absent, that it is just a performance.

Last month I saw a performance of Shakespeare's play *The Tempest*, which is also about illusion and reality; and later I saw Peter Greenaway's film *Prospero's Books*. Prospero, the exiled Duke of Milan, has spent his life studying magic, and by his magic he entices on to his enchanted isle a shipload of people, including those who have most wronged him: his brother who usurped his Dukedom, and the King of Naples who assisted him. The play starts with a shipwreck, but we realise later that this is not real, but an illusion created by Prospero. Then the people wander around, not knowing whether they are waking or dreaming, but all the time being manipulated by Prospero.

He can do what he likes with them. What tricks will he not play on his enemies who are now in his power?

He determines to forgive them. That is the surprising thing in the play. He decides to forgive, and by that forgiveness he sets them free and sets himself free. And to do that he must abandon the magic which gives him his power over them, his ability to manipulate them.

> *This rough magic*
> *I here abjure ...*
>  *I'll break my staff,*
> *Bury it certain fathoms in the earth,*
> *And, deeper than did ever plummet sound,*
> *I'll drown my book.*

Prospero's guests, wandering in a trance in his enchanted island, and wandering also in the evil thoughts and devices of their hearts, find reality through his forgiveness, and find their true selves in the process: as Gonzalo puts it, they have found 'All of us ourselves, When no man was his own.' They are set free.

And in the epilogue to the play, Prospero himself takes leave of his audience and asks their forgiveness:

> *As you from crimes would pardoned be*
> *Let your indulgence set me free.*

There is reality. All else is illusion.

To come back, as a preacher should, to where I started, I realise that Virtual Reality may have good uses—architects are becoming excited about it, and some doctors. But what is it about that strange new technique for creating an artificial experience that makes it ultimately unreal? Why, just this: that to experience Virtual Reality I must be alone, isolated, in a room by myself. The greatest illusion is to imagine that you are the only person in the universe. The ultimate reality, which frees us from illusion, is love and forgiveness. God is the ultimate reality, and God is love.

# 7

# Religion as Bargain and Religion as Love

*Readings:* Hosea 6:1-6; Matthew 9:1-13

*Text:* Hosea 6:6

> *For I desire steadfast love and not sacrifice, the knowledge of God rather than burnt offerings.*

The Scots are not, like the Welsh, thought of as great singers, yet deep in the hearts of most Presbyterian Scots—of my generation anyway—lie the greatest of the Psalms and Paraphrases that we have sung from our youth. Many of us regret that only a selection of these is available to us in our present hymn-book.

But one that no compiler could omit was what we used to know as the 30th Paraphrase:

> *Come, let us to the Lord our God*
> *With contrite hearts return;*
> *Our God is gracious, nor will leave*
> *The desolate to mourn.*

Paraphrase 30 is a beautiful devotional poem which has expressed the penitence and the trust of generations of our forefathers.

The surprising thing then is to realise that the passage on which it is based, Hosea 6:1-3, was not intended by its author to be read as a model of deep and sincere religion. It is rather given as an example of the kind of religion that drives God to despair.

Let me read the first four verses of Hosea 6 again. The first three verses represent a liturgical song, sung at a religious service, when sacrifice was made:

*Come, let us return to the Lord;*
*for he has torn that he may heal us;*
*he has stricken and he will bind us up.*
*After two days he will revive us;*
*on the third day he will raise us up,*
*that we may live before him.*
*Let us know, let us press on to know the Lord;*
*his going forth is sure as the dawn*
*he will come to us as the showers,*
*as the spring rains that water the earth.*

And God's response is:

*What shall I do with you, O Ephraim?*
*What shall I do with you, O Judah?*
*Your love is like a morning cloud,*
*like the dew that goes early away.*

This turning to God is a knee-jerk reaction to danger, and when the danger is past, where will this new-found devotion be? Vanished like the dew.

As the prophet saw it, there were two dangers facing his people. The external danger was the danger of invasion from the rising empire of Assyria in the north east. That did, in fact, happen.

The internal threat—as Hosea saw it the more important—was that they were allowing their religion to be corrupted by the religion of the land, the cult of Baal.

Israel's faith in Yahweh, their name for the one and only God, had been born in the desert when they were nomadic herdsmen, under the open sky. When they settled to become farmers in Palestine, they found that the whole cycle of farming activity among their neighbours was punctuated by rituals and sacrifices to the Gods of the land—the Baalim—to secure fertility and good harvests. The received farming wisdom was, 'You won't get a good harvest unless you sacrifice to Baal.'

Elijah had contended against the priests of Baal, in an attempt to call Israel back to the pure worship of Yahweh. But the pull of superstition is always strong with the human race—the belief that good luck follows if you perform certain rituals and bad luck if you omit them. So Baal worship and sacrifice was always insidiously taking over Israel's religion.

Here in the little song at the beginning of chapter 6, it is as if Israel had responded to Hosea's preaching. Perhaps they were scared by the threat of an Assyrian invasion. Anyhow, they have decided to do as Hosea asked, and turn to the true God, to Yahweh, and away from the false Gods, the Baalim. 'Come, let us return to Yahweh.' And later, in verse 3, 'Let us know, let us press on to know Yahweh.' (Incidentally, whenever in the Authorised Version or Revised Standard Version of the Old Testament you find the word LORD in capital letters, behind that lies the Hebrew name for God, 'Yahweh'.)

Now to turn back to Yahweh was just what Hosea had been asking them to do. So that's all right surely? Why should not Yahweh accept this little liturgy of penitence?

The answer is, I think, that although the language is all right the attitude is all wrong. The language is the language of the worship of the true God, but the attitude is the attitude of Baal worship. Pagan worship was essentially a kind of magic, a belief that if you perform the right sacrifices in the right way, hey presto, the desired results will follow. So, in a sense, you had the God in your power. He would do what you wanted if you made the right sacrifice. And here in this little hymn, the people of Israel are turning not to Baal but to Yahweh, but they're carrying the attitudes of Baal into their worship. They think they have God in their pocket.

'He has torn that he may heal us; he has stricken and he will bind us up.' God's response to their prayer will be automatic. It will be as sure as the changes in the seasons. We've made our sacrifice and everything will be all right now.

This is slot-machine religion. You put in your money and out comes the bar of chocolate. It is also cupboard love. It is religion as bargain. 'We'll turn to God—he'll see we're all right.'

And God says what can I do with a religion like that? It has no depth to it. It's like a morning mist, which disappears when the sun gets up.

My people have not understood. 'For I desire steadfast love and not sacrifice, the knowledge of God, rather than burnt offerings.'

What we have here then is a contrast between two kinds of religion: religion as love and religion as bargain.

Now it is not just Baal worship which thinks of religion as like an automatic vending machine, where you put in the right money, press the right buttons, and God will deliver the goods. It is very natural to all of us to want to reduce religion to that kind of assurance: we do the right things, go through the right motions and God will do as we ask. Practically the whole of medieval religion was of this kind, and a great deal of Christian teaching then and since—attitudes to the sacraments and to prayer, for instance. And we are all very apt to reduce religion to an implicit bargain with God—if we live a good life (that is our version of sacrifice) then God will be good to us. And we can feel very let

41

down if he doesn't seem to be keeping his end of the bargain. I've always lived a good life, why should this suffering, this sorrow, happen to me? And sometimes we can feel even more let down if someone who doesn't deserve it, someone who has never tried, as we have, to be good, seems to bask in God's favour. Whenever we feel like that, our religion has become a bargain, and God doesn't seem to be keeping the bargain.

But God doesn't want commercial religion, religion as bargain. He wants religion as love:

*Go and learn what this means, 'I desire mercy, and not sacrifice.'*

These words are spoken by Jesus, quoting Hosea 6:6, and they're spoken to the Pharisees. And the Pharisees have been complaining because Jesus is not sticking to the bargain. It is the good people who deserve God's favour, and the Pharisees are the good people. They have a right to God's love: others have none. But Jesus is eating and drinking with the tax collectors and the sinners. He is telling them that God loves them. He is telling them that their sins are forgiven. He has even called some to be his disciples. This is to break the bargain which is the whole basis of their religion. And Jesus says, 'Go and learn what this means, "I desire mercy, and not sacrifice".'

In other words, not the religion of the bargain, but the religion of love. 'Mercy' is one translation of a word which in our Old Testament passage is translated 'steadfast love'—'I desire steadfast love and not sacrifice.'

A world which is dominated, as ours is, by commercial relationships, finds it hard to understand love. Those who believe that money can buy anything tend to believe you can buy love. You can't. Love is free. It's free in two senses. In the sense that you don't and can't pay for it. It's given, not bought.

And it's free also in the sense that love is liberty. It is free. It's not compelled, it's not constrained. You cannot, as a friend said to me, twist someone's arm to make them love you.

Even the impassioned question 'Do you love me?' may evoke the response 'Yes, I love you', but can such a reluctant confession dispel the lack of trust that lies behind the question in the first place? Love is given freely.

So is the love of God. It is given freely, and it is not for us to dictate to him whom he should love and whom despise. It is given freely and we need not pretend that we deserve it. It is given freely, and we can be sure—for we have seen it in Christ—that it is with us whether we are basking in the sunshine or cowering in the rain, whether our heart is light with joy or heavy with sadness and pain. The Father loved the Son no less when he hung in agony on the cross than when he sat in comfort at the dinner tables of the tax-collectors—or of the Pharisees, for he was guest to both indifferently.

When we understand the steadfastness of God's love, its joy and its pain, and know that we live only by his grace and in his forgiveness, then something of that steadfast love is formed in us, and we throw away the silly bargains that we make with life, and enjoy instead the freedom of those who love.

The faith is there in the 30th Paraphrase, and it has transformed the little song of Hosea into a song of gratitude for God's unlimited grace.

# 8

# Choose Life

SERVICE OF RE-DEDICATION OF A CHURCH

*Readings:* Deuteronomy 30:11-20; Philippians 4:4-9;
Matthew 6:24-34

*Text:* Deuteronomy 30:19

> *I call heaven and earth to witness against you this day, that I
> have set before you life and death, blessing and curse; there-
> fore choose life ...*

We often hear it said that the Church is not buildings, but people:
and, of course, that is important and correct. The Church is not a
building, but a fellowship. God is not a building, nor does he
dwell in buildings, but in the hearts of men and women.

And yet, as I travel around the Church—and in the past few
years I've been in a good many different churches—I find that
the state of the church buildings very often gives me a clue as to
the spiritual state of the congregation. When I find a church that
is shabby, dirty, with piles of old dog-eared hymn-books and
Bibles without covers, I guess that there is here a congregation
that is dispirited, down-hearted and without hope. When I find a
church that is well-looked after, well-kept, a building that is loved,
my guess is that there is a congregation here that loves the worship
of God and rejoices in his service. And my guesses have usually
proved right. For what we do with the material things that are
given us—whether we create beauty or dinginess—is a good sign

of the health or sickness of our spirits. Here, you have used good materials to create something of beauty and of worth, a place not only to be a home for your congregation but a place that is welcoming to the many who now belong to no congregation at all.

I don't know if any of you will remember Dennis Potter's Television play, *Son of Man*. It was regarded as controversial when it was originally shown more than twenty years ago. But I warmed to the late Colin Blakeley's portrayal of a Jesus who was not cold and aloof as so often in our religious films, but direct, spontaneous, warm, human. In Potter's play, we saw Jesus thinking on his feet as he taught, appealing to his hearers, hugging them around the shoulders, inviting them to share his vision, his enthusiasm. I like to think that Jesus was like that.

There was one scene in the play that had no basis in the Gospels —it was a piece of pure imagination. That was a scene where Jesus and the disciples chance on a place of execution where some criminals, or rebels, have been crucified, and they are now taking the bodies down from the cross.

The crowds slowly disperse, leaving the empty crosses, but the disciples linger at this scene of horror, all of them moved and awed by it. Jesus, in an anguish of emotion at the callousness and the cruelty of men, puts his arms round the cross, and hides his face against it. Then it is as if the carpenter in him takes over, and his hands are telling him something, and he stands back in surprise.

This is good timber. Look at that. Straight from the heart of the tree. Not a knot in it. You could split that straight ... make tables and chairs.

Then he begins to laugh, and the disciples are mystified. 'Think of it,' he says. 'God gives the seed, and it goes into the soil and God feeds it by the sun and the rain, and it grows. God gives more sun, more rain, years pass, and it's a tall tree. Then men come and cut it down with an axe. Nothing wrong with that. God gives it for our use. We can make tables, chairs, good things, useful things. But what do men make? A cross!'

That scene, that piece of pure imagining, has stuck in my mind since I first saw it. The Carpenter of Nazareth, admiring the timber of which a cross was made, and wondering, in a horrified sadness, that men, given such good material, make from it— a cross.

Look at the world today—at what you read in the papers or see on the television news—and ask why is it that the human race, given so many blessings, turns them into curses? Given the choice of life and good, we choose instead death and evil? Why, from the wonderful timber of a tree, make the ugly torture of a cross?

Why do the landowners and farmers of Colombia, who might grow food to bring life to the poor people of their land, choose instead to grow drugs that deal death to the young people of other lands? Why do the nations, all with many hungry mouths to feed, and families poorly housed, choose instead to spend their wealth on weapons of mass destruction?

'See, I have set before you this day life and death, blessing and curse. Therefore choose life.'

Why don't we? Why don't we?

That is the mystery of human sin, and perhaps there is no answer to the question 'Why?', because to choose evil rather than good, death rather than life, is irrational.

It is not as if this was some esoteric wisdom, revealed only to the initiates. You don't need to pierce the heavens for this truth or send someone over the sea to some Eastern guru. 'The word is very near you; it is in your mouth and in your heart, so that you can do it.' We know in our heart that life is better than death, love than hate, kindness than cruelty, good than evil. We know in our heart that we are called to create not destroy, to cherish life and not

46

to kill it. But it doesn't require any cleverness to see that. You don't need a university degree to understand it. It should be obvious to anyone that this is the way the world is.

Why then do we choose the opposite? Lots of explanations have been given, and I'm not going to go into them here. Because I think they all fail to pierce the mystery of iniquity—why it is that, given the good timber of a tree, men should fashion it into a cross.

Yet that is what we do, and the evidence is all around us. It is a cruel and a destructive world in which we live. Herbert Butterfield, the historian and Christian believer, said, 'What history does is to uncover man's universal sin', which is an echo of Edward Gibbon, who said, 'History is little more than the register of the crimes, follies and misfortunes of mankind.' Today it is not so much the history book as the television screen that gives us all the register of crime, folly and misfortune that we need.

Given good timber, men still make it into a cross. The destruction of rain forests in India, Africa and South America is the main cause of flooding and famine and the spread of the desert. Why is the timber cut? Not to make tables and chairs and useful things, but for greed—to exploit the land and to clear the ground so that it can grow cash crops to sell to the rich countries in exchange for arms, or to help pay the crippling debt that they already owe to these rich countries. Reckless greed and reckless aggression take the fruitful field and make of it a desert.

Saddam Hussein believed that civilisation equals military might. So he spent his oil wealth on weapons of mass destruction—the materials for which Russia and the West and we here in Britain have willingly traded with him. Saddam might have used the money and the high technology to reclaim the desert and to feed his people. But he chose death.

Jesus said, 'You cannot serve God and Money', and that is as

47

modern a version of 'Therefore choose life' as anyone can wish. It is a matter of which God people worship. Do we love and serve the God who gives us every blessing, or do we worship money, possession, grabbing all we can, no matter what the consequences for our world or our children's world? Along that road lies the 'weary, soiled earth', the polluted planet.

But it is possible for mankind to choose life. If we treat with respect the good things God has given us, and take seriously the needs of others, then the blessings of God follow, and the desert may again become fruitful field, and the world be secure for our children and our children's children.

It is possible for mankind to choose life. Against the God of greed and grab, who is the dominant deity in our society there have always been those who witness to the God of justice and humanity. But are they to remain only the relief workers of this world—the Red Cross, Oxfam and Christian Aid trying to get food and medical supplies through to starving people while civil war rages around them? Can we move Governments to be concerned about people instead of money and power? Perhaps we can. The European Commission is pressing on Governments to clean up our beaches and our rivers and our seas which have been polluted by our human and our industrial and our nuclear waste. It can be done and it must be done and it is beginning to be done. Can we also take action about the depletion of the ozone layer, to limit the emissions that cause the damage? Action cannot be delayed forever, if this planet is to be a pleasant place for our children to live in.

Some years ago the Thames was so dirty that if you fell in they took you to hospital to pump you out. Recently there have been fish again in the Thames—because the then Thames Water Board and the Greater London Council put their heads and their hearts together and cleaned the river up. We have the power, if we still have the political will, to make this world sweet for human life.

'Therefore choose life.' Why is it that given the choice between life and death, we so often choose death? Why are we so often destructive, rather than creative? Why, given a rich world to live in, do we plunder it; a fine planet and we pollute it? Why, given good timber, do we choose not things of beauty, but squalor, destruction and death?

But you have taken good materials in this church, and have used them, not for greed or for aggrandisement, but for the glory and the worship of God. God's blessings allowed to sing to his praise. You have taken material things and used them to create a place of new beauty—not just for yourselves but for the worship of God in this place in time to come. And in that, it seems to me, you witness to your faith, the Gospel that is preached here Sunday by Sunday.

For the final mystery is not 'Why do men take good timber and make of it a cross?' The ultimately mysterious question is 'How can God take a Cross and make of it the means of our salvation?' How can the cross, a symbol of man's cruelty and hatred, suffering and death, become a symbol of life triumphant over death, of good triumphant over evil, of love triumphant over hate, of forgiveness reaching even to the unforgivable?

We sing:

*Nothing in my hand I bring,*
*Simply to thy cross I cling.*

And when we do just that, we find it to be good timber indeed, for here the suffering God reaches down to us in blessing, to redeem all sinful, suffering humanity, and to offer us again, as a gift, the life that we have so often failed to choose for ourselves.

# 9

# Room for All

A COMMUNION SERMON

*Lessons:* Isaiah 25:1-9; Luke 14:12-24

*Text:* Luke 14:22

> *And the servant said, 'Sir, what you commanded has been done, and still there is room.'*

It seems natural among human beings that when they have something to celebrate they celebrate with a feast. You find this in all societies and in all levels of society. And we are no exception. We like to have Christmas dinner. At birthdays there is a cake. Perhaps even on Fathers' Day, there will be something special for tea. Next month, at the university graduations, the hotels and restaurants here in St Andrews will be full of families having a celebratory lunch, with a bottle of wine for those not driving.

In the Old Testament you find plenty of stories of how kings and great ones celebrated their victories, or whatever else they had to celebrate, by giving a feast. And it was natural that those Jews who looked forward to the coming of God's kingdom, the real victory of God over all that is evil, should think of that as being celebrated with a feast.

Isaiah looked forward to it. 'On this mountain [that is, in Jerusalem] the Lord of Hosts will make for all people a feast of fat things, of fat things full of marrow, of wine on the lees well refined.' Isaiah clearly had not heard of chloresterol, but his meaning is clear. The very best that can be provided, the best of food and drink that you could imagine—that's what it will be like in God's kingdom.

It was that thought that prompted a fellow-guest, sitting with Jesus at a dinner-party, to say, 'Blessed is he who shall eat bread in the Kingdom of God.' It was a pious thought, designed, no doubt, to impress Jesus, as if to say, 'Here I am, tucking into my dinner like everyone else, but my mind is on higher things.' Perhaps he expected Jesus to praise him. It was the sort of remark that is very difficult to disagree with. As if someone today were to say, 'We need more prayer.' How do you answer that? I used to hear that remark interjected into ecumenical study-groups, and I often felt like answering, 'No, we need less prayer, and less pious sentiment, and a bit more common-sense.' But I don't know if I ever had the courage.

Jesus did though. His answer to the pious sentiment was to tell a story which may well have made his fellow-guest wish he'd kept his big mouth shut. This story we know as the Parable of the Great Feast.

And it is a story of those who have been invited to a feast and don't want to go. They make excuses. They can't afford the time for anything as frivolous as a party. There are pressing business concerns to be attended to—I've bought land and I have to go and survey it, measure out the boundaries and see that they are clearly marked; I've bought livestock and I have to attend to them, and see that they are in good shape, or else I'll want my money back. So please have me excused.

And there was a pressing domestic concern which brooked no argument. I have married a wife, and therefore I cannot come.

Many young married couples have felt like that. There was a law in ancient Israel which said, 'When a man is newly married, he shall not go out with the army or be charged with any business;

51

he shall be free at home one year, to be happy with his wife whom he has taken.' A very humane provision, and perhaps that was what was being pleaded as an excuse for not coming to the great feast—though a feast could hardly be classed as war or business.

No matter, for the point of the story, which is what makes it, like so many of Jesus' parables, an unlikely and even ridiculous story, is that they all made such excuses. None of the people who were invited came to the feast. And Jesus is saying, 'That's what the Kingdom of God is like—God is offering a feast, and those whom he invites stay away. God offers laughter and joy and celebration, and people are afraid of it.'

Why? Well, in human terms, the real reason behind the excuses is often that you don't want to be obliged. Perhaps the people in the parable had learned too well the saying, 'There is no such thing as a free meal.' To accept someone's hospitality puts you under an obligation, either to repay the hospitality or to accept that you can't repay it, because he is much richer and stronger than you, and to go to his party would be to acknowledge your dependence on him.

There are many households in this town, I'm sure, who arrange their hospitality through a little list. 'We'd better have the Smiths in, because they invited us, and we haven't had them back yet.' Sometimes that seems a little calculating, but it is natural enough between equals—a debt of gratitude which you are happy to pay.

But there are other situations when you can't do this. Many ministers through the years have preached at Crathie and enjoyed the hospitality of Her Majesty the Queen at Balmoral. Now it doesn't occur to them, when they write their respectful bread-and-butter letters, to suggest that perhaps Her Majesty would like to come and spend a week-end with them sometime. The Queen's hospitality is hospitality that you cannot repay, except, perhaps, with your love and your loyalty.

Is this the point of the parable? People don't want to accept a free gift from God. Either because they can't trust his generosity, or because they'd rather have a business relationship with God —a you-scratch-my-back-and-I'll-scratch-yours arrangement. They can't cope with the idea of a God who simply invites you to a feast.

Jesus came with the good news of a loving and forgiving God, a God whom we can call Father. The good news of a generous God, a God who invites, accepts, receives us, who offers us life. This message is there in his parables—the Prodigal Son, the Lost Sheep. But the cold-hearted religion of so many of his people couldn't cope with this warm-hearted God.

For they had their religion worked out. It was a kind of business. The bargain was that if they kept the law, then they would earn the kingdom. And they were very serious and very scrupulous about it.

And they were very critical of people who didn't keep the law as scrupulously as they did. And to be told that they didn't need to earn the kingdom, couldn't indeed earn the kingdom, they had to receive it as a gift, an invitation to a feast—that was too much for them.

But what followed was even worse. For if they weren't keen to accept God's gift of grace, other people were. But these were the very people that the unco guid despised. Some who had lost the way and found themselves in the gutter. Some who had made terrible mistakes in their youth, which they regretted ever since. Some who had got into wrong company, and played dangerous games. Some who had been ground into poverty and couldn't believe that anyone cared about them. They knew they couldn't earn the kingdom. They'd given up trying long since. Now they were being invited in, and they were coming to the feast of God's love, the feast of his forgiveness.

The tax-gatherers and the sinners heard Jesus gladly. Good news about God, good news about forgiveness was what they needed to hear, and no one but Jesus brought it to them. That's there in the parable. For when the invited guests don't come, the master does not cancel his feast. Instead, he sends his servant out to the streets and lanes of the city to bring in the poor and maimed and blind and lame. Beggars, probably all of them. They don't have any difficulty about accepting his invitation. They know he can't expect them to ask him back. And a free meal is a free meal—especially when you're hungry.

The servant comes back and says, 'Sir, what you commanded has been done, and still there is room.'

Then the master said to the servant, 'Go out to the highways and hedges and compel people to come in, that my house may be filled.'

The injunction to bring them in by the scruff of the neck was perhaps just a vivid way of showing the master's passionate desire that there shouldn't be a vacant place at his table. For Luke I think it represented also the Gentile mission of the Church. The servant goes first to the streets and lanes of the city—*ie* to Israel—and then to the highways and hedges, outside of the city—*ie* to the Gentiles.

Now there's clearly a connection between the bringing in of the poor and maimed and blind and lame, and the advice Jesus had given earlier to the host who had invited him:

*When you give a dinner or a banquet, don't invite your friends or your brothers or your kinsmen or rich neighbours, in case they invite you back, and you are repaid. But when you give a feast invite the poor, the maimed, the lame, the blind, and you will be blessed because they cannot repay you.*

This whole story sets before us two contrasting attitudes to life and religion. One sees life in terms of deals and bargains, of paying and being repaid. Everything is exactly measured, and what you get and what you give is precisely what is deserved, no more, no less.

The other sees life in terms of generosity and acceptance. Of giving, without wondering when you will be repaid, and of receiving, without spoiling it all by thinking, 'When will I ever be able to pay this back?'

It's not difficult to see that the second is the way of life, the way of enjoyment. It is that way of life and religion that Jesus offers us. For God is the generous giver. When we come to the feast of love and forgiveness which we know we haven't deserved, we can learn to be generous to others, without asking too precisely who deserves what in this life.

The food and the drink at our communion services are tokens of a feast. But there is nothing formal about the love which is proclaimed under these tokens of bread and wine. The boundless love of God, inviting us to the feast of his kingdom.

And, such is his generosity, that at his table and in his heart there is always room. Room for us, and room for all those for whom his heart still yearns.

*Sir, what you commanded has been done, and still there is room.*

# 10

# Young Simeon

*Readings:* Isaiah 52:1-10;
Luke 2:22-38

*Text:* Luke 2:29-32

> *Lord, now lettest thou thy servant depart in peace, according to thy word; for mine eyes have seen thy salvation which thou hast prepared in the presence of all peoples, a light for revelation to the Gentiles, and for glory to thy people Israel.*

At the beginning of my ministry, when I was an army chaplain, I was for a time Presbyterian chaplain at a depot where there was fine Anglican church, and two Anglican chaplains to serve it. I was able to use the church for my Presbyterian service, in between their early morning Communion and their eleven o'clock Mattins. And on the Sunday evening they always had Evensong, and for that service, as for Mattins, they had a fine choir. And quite often they used to invite me to preach at Evensong. I thought it was very gracious of them to ask me, though I think they were quite happy to get out of writing another sermon.

Anyhow I loved doing it, because I loved Evensong. Every Sunday evening we sang the Magnificat, the triumphant song of Mary, 'My soul doth magnify the Lord .... ' One Sunday I was enjoying it so much, I quite forgot to go forward to read the New Testament lesson. Then, after the New Testament lesson, we sang the *Nunc Dimittis*, the quieter song of Simeon: 'Lord now lettest thou thy servant depart in peace.'

And I can't hear these songs now without thinking of these far-off days at the Guards' Depot.

So now I turn again to these familiar words: 'Lord, now lettest thou thy servant depart in peace.' Strange, when you come to think of it, that I should come to love them when I was still very young—I was only 26 at that time—because we think of this as an old man's song. Though there's nothing in Luke's Gospel to say that Simeon was old:

*Now there was a man in Jerusalem, whose name was Simeon, and this man was righteous and devout, looking for the consolation of Israel, and the Holy Spirit was upon him.*

Luke doesn't say he was an old man, yet everyone assumes he was.

Is this one of those cases where we read more into the New Testament than is actually there? Ask any Sunday School child about the wise men in Matthew, and she'll tell you that there were three and that they were kings, and many even give you their names. But Matthew says only that wise men came, doesn't say how many—there might have been a dozen—and certainly not that they were kings. That comes from the nativity plays and from the carols, and also perhaps from the neat idea that if they gave gold and frankincense and myrrh, that's one gift each.

So we take these uncanny stories from the New Testament, which already have a legendary character—they're not newspaper reports, that's for sure—and we add our own trimmings, which aren't in the New Testament at all. So when you read the second chapter of Matthew, you're not seeing what is written there—you are seeing three strangely dignified young boys, wearing card-

57

board crowns, clad in their father's silk dressing-gowns, bearing their caskets and singing, 'We three kings of Orient are.' The Bible hasn't a chance.

Now to come back to Simeon. He had the great good fortune not to get written into the nativity play, but we imagine him as old, though the Bible doesn't say so.

Those of you who are old enough to remember the Scottish Paraphrases may remember that Paraphrase 46 began, 'Just and devout old Simeon lived.' I looked up a commentary on Luke's Gospel, and found that the commentator also assumed that Simeon was old. Yet try as I may, I can find nothing in the New Testament to say so.

Perhaps it's his association with Hannah, for she was certainly old and Luke is at pains to tell us. I don't know why Luke stresses her age. He must have had a reason. But he does not refer to Simeon's age at all.

Perhaps everyone has assumed that Simeon was old because of the nature of his song. 'Lord, now lettest thou thy servant depart in peace.'

'I'm ready to go, Lord, any time you like.' Now I've often felt like that: but then I am an old man. I've had my three-score years and ten. I'm living on borrowed time, as they used to say. Sometimes I say that in faith—I know I must die sometime, and when the time comes I hope I'll welcome it. 'Lord now lettest thou thy servant .... '

But really, to think of Simeon's song in that way is to miss the point. So let's put Simeon's age out of the reckoning. He may have been 26, as I was when I first learned to love his song. He may have been 70, he may have been anything in between. He is a man, an adult human being. And he is just and devout, looking for the consolation of Israel.

In the times when Simeon was living, you might say that God

didn't seem to have been doing very much recently. It wasn't a new experience for the Jews, for centuries before they had been transported from their own country into captivity in Babylon, and there for long years they had waited and wondered whether and when their God would do anything to save them. Some of their songs of complaint we have in the Psalms, and their attempts to keep their faith alive in the dark times of their exile. 'Lord, how long?' they cried, as they longed to be back in Jerusalem. And some of the prophets saw the promise of their return. The passage we read, Isaiah 52, is one such wonderful promise that God will act to restore Israel and set the captives free.

Now Babylon or Babylonia is pretty familiar to us today. For the country they knew as Babylonia is more or less the modern Iraq, and the city of Babylon was a little to the south of modern Baghdad. So what we have seen with such thankfulness in the recent past is the end of a little Babylonian captivity. But our captives, the hostages, were held for only months, thank God, not for a whole lifetime.

But God in his grace—freely, or our old Testament passage keeps repeating—liberated his people from Babylon, and it was through the Persian empire—Iran—thrusting west and setting them free.

And at the time of Jesus, they were back in their own land, but not free, not independent, under the heel of the Romans. And the priestly class, the Sadducees, had settled for collaboration with the occupying forces, and were doing quite well out of it. And their rivals, the Pharisees, had made the law their own God —the way some people make the Bible their God today—and they put all their energies into scrupulous observance of the law. But there was a group, possibly of very humble people, certainly without power, who read the stories of what God had done for Israel in the past, and the great prophecies of the last chapters of

59

Isaiah, and who waited, hoped, expected, longed for, prayed for the day when God would once again, in his own way, liberate his people, restore to them the independence which they had lost so many years before.

To that group Simeon and the aged Hannah both belonged. So here was a man, a patriot and a devout believer, whose whole being was bound up in, focussed on the expectation that God would restore Israel and liberate Jerusalem. And somehow, I don't know how (how does one know these things? The Holy Spirit, Luke says, had told him), he knew in his heart of hearts, that he was going to see it some day, it was going to happen in his lifetime this deliverance which had become the aim and purpose of his life.

And one day this man comes into the temple, his mind full of this as it always was, and he catches sight of a poor couple who have come to make the offering required by the law, a thank-offering for their first-born son. They're just poor people, making the offering that was allowed by the law for those who couldn't afford a lamb.

Poor people, not worthy of a second glance. But his eye stops on them, and suddenly (how does one know these things? Luke says the Holy Spirit told him) he knows, knows in his heart of hearts that this is it. This is what he has been waiting for. He takes the child from the astonished parents, and pours out his thanks-giving: 'Lord, now lettest thou thy servant depart in peace, according to thy word, for mine eyes have seen thy salvation.' And in his song he echoes phrases from Isaiah 52 and other prophecies, to shout that this is something for the whole world to see, the culmination of the story of Israel. 'Thy salvation which thou hast prepared in the presence of all peoples, to be a light for revelation to the Gentiles, and for glory to thy people Israel.'

This is no world-weary sigh for release from a wicked world.

It's a song of triumph every bit as much as Mary's. This is a man who has found what he's been looking for. He can die happy now, because he knows everything's all right. God has acted and will act.

We don't know if he died then or if he lived for years, boring everyone with the story of his great experience in the temple. He disappears from Luke's story just as mysteriously as he enters it.

But from Luke's point of view, he has served his purpose. First, he represents the poor and powerless people of the world, who have no power to do anything, but can only wait and hope and suffer and watch and pray.

There were many poor and powerless in the world, as there are now. And to the faithful ones who don't give up looking for a better world, it is given to see the sign, the promise of the better way that is to be.

Second, for Luke, Simeon shows that God's salvation is where you least expect it:

*They all were looking for a king,*
*to slay their foes and lift them high.*
*Thou camest, a little baby thing,*
*that made a woman cry.*

Supposing there had been a leadership election going on among the Sadducees, with all the media concentrating on it and the *Jerusalem Times* interviewing all the candidates, and the Pharisees a bit miffed that their rivals were getting all this publicity. If such things had been possible in Jerusalem, you might have been excused for thinking, 'This is where the action is. Perhaps here is the new start we're looking for.' Well mebbe aye and mebbe no, but on that occasion the action was where nobody was looking—in two poor parents bringing their child to the temple.

They must all have thought the man was mad to take a baby up in his arms and say, 'Now, at last, I've seen the salvation of God.' Perhaps the parents were relieved to get the child back in their arms again. Oh yes, he'd seen that this was no ordinary child. But to see God's salvation there in the weakness and helplessness of the child, that was vision indeed.

Perhaps that's what Luke wants us to ask. Where do we look for the salvation of God? In the infant in the temple, the growing boy among the teachers, the carpenter in his workshop, the preacher of good news, the young man dying on a cross, falsely accused. Where do we look today? In the same sort of place. In the innocence of childish trust, in the love of truth and of work well done, in the love that forgives, in the faith that endures. We see the Lord's Christ in the things the world despises, in the courage that is trampled underfoot.

Where do we see the salvation of God? Young Simeon knew, and in a dark world uttered a cry of hope.

# 11

# Love never ends

*Readings:* Isaiah 40:21-31; 1 Corinthians 13

*Text:* 1 Corinthians 13:8

*Love never ends.*

There was a great deal of fuss in the newspapers and on television about the end of the last decade.

I happen to be one of those purists who believe that a decade ends at the end of the tenth year, and that a century ends at the end of the hundredth year, and that a millennium is fulfilled at the end of the thousandth year, not at the end of the nine hundred and ninety-ninth. But we purists are in a minority, and the pressure of the popular press and of television is very strong, and I suppose we have to bow in the end to the popular will. So, if I'm spared, as they say, I will probably celebrate the end of the century and of the millennium, seven years from now, along with everybody else.

But what's so big about the end of a decade, or a century, or a millennium for that matter? 'For a thousand years in thy sight are but as yesterday when it is past, or as a watch in the night,' says the Psalmist. The tens, the hundreds and the thousands are our human ways of measuring time. They give us the illusion of control over this inexorable dimension in which we live. But from the Divine perspective, they may look very different indeed.

We don't need to go as far as the Divine perspective—the geologist can make our decades look very small indeed. When I visited the Geology department of one of our universities, I was given a fossil, a trilobite, and was told it was 450 million years old. So when, later, I was able to show it to my son, I said, 'That fossil is 450 million years and one month old.'

That, of course, confuses geological and human time. Geological time knows only millions of years. Our counting of our brief days and months and years is important because it measures out our human life, as the counting of centuries measures out our human history.

Our western culture is very much aware of change, and therefore of time's passing. Ask a modern child 'How old are you?' and you will get the answer 'Four' or 'Seven', and sometimes with great precision, 'Five and three-quarters.' But in other cultures there is less awareness of time, other than of the rhythms of nature. Ask a man when he was born, and he is liable to think for a minute and say 'in the winter'.

Time for us is a mystery. It is there before we are born. We have our brief life. Time goes on, but we are no longer in it. Like a river, it flows inexorably in one direction, and can never go back. Time reminds us of our mortality.

I remember a little verse on the phrase 'to kill time', in which Time is the speaker:

*There's nothing upon which mankind agree*
*So much as in their boast of killing me.*
*I boast of nothing. Yet, when I've a mind,*
*I think I can be even with mankind.*

We think time is at our disposal, yet, at the end of the day, it is time that disposes of us. It was Protestantism, oddly enough, that first began to take time seriously. In the Middle Ages, this life was seen solely as the preparation for the next, and the only important business was to save one's soul. In the monasteries, to which those seriously intent on the saving of their souls repaired in large numbers, the business of prayer required the division of the day into hours. Monks got up in the middle of the night to pray, so that Satan would have less opportunity to tempt them to naughty thoughts or deeds. So a clock was necessary to tell the hours. But in the world of agriculture or commerce, the sun and the seasons gave all the calendar that most people needed. And so it is in many countries today.

But Protestantism took this world and its business seriously, and believed that God wants us to serve him in this world, using that time that he gives us. Time then became a precious gift of God, and it was a sin to waste it in idleness. Protestant Geneva became a centre for the making of clocks and watches, of an accuracy only now surpassed by the ubiquitous invention of the quartz mechanism. You glorified God by the way you used the precious gift of time, not primarily to make yourself rich, but to be useful to our community and to your neighbour.

Protestantism was always inclined to be too serious, and not to allow that life was sometimes simply to be enjoyed, and time a gift of God to be enjoyed to his glory.

But a strange thing has happened today. Protestant faith refers our life to God and sees the time that is given to us as a blessing of his providing. With the decline in that faith today, it is as if the Protestant attitude to time has been exaggerated and distorted into a grotesque parody. People live their lives with their eye on that watch that loses no more than a second a year. Our world seems to be divided into two. There are the unemployed and the elderly, who may well have time on their hands. There are those who are going places, or hope they are going places, and they are always in a hurry. It is not that they don't have leisure. But that is lived at the same time intensity as their working life, with the same exhausting seriousness. And the symbols of their success are their expensive toys, houses, cars, yachts, whatever.

And such people are the heroes of our time, to be envied, to be emulated. When a Cabinet minister resigned because he wanted more time to spend with his young family, I applauded him, if that was really the reason for his resignation. But nobody seems to have asked about the situation from which he was extricating himself. It seems to be accepted that the demands of office put great strain on families. But would we not be a lot better governed if Cabinet ministers didn't have to work at that pace and under such pressure? And who sets the pace and the pressure? I doubt if it's all that necessary.

And I begin to ask a question. If we no longer see our time as a precious gift of God, and our life as overshadowed and renewed and upheld by the Lord, who is the Everlasting God, the Creator of the ends of the earth, who faints not neither is weary, if we lose that faith in the God who transcends time and is the Lord of time—what do we substitute for it?

I was thinking about this when I looked again at the passage I had chosen for the Old Testament lesson this morning. I chose it for the magnificent description of the God who transcends time. 'Have you not known? Have you not heard? The Lord is the everlasting God, the Creator of the ends of the earth.' Then I looked at the reason why these things were being said. Chapter 40 of Isaiah really begins a new book, by a prophet who was speaking to the Jews in exile in Babylon, and bringing them comfort, and renewing their faith. And it seems that many of the captives in Babylon felt that they had been deserted by their God, that he was no longer interested in them, or that he had in fact been defeated. They had lost faith. And one reaction to that was to say, 'Well, we'd better come to terms with the Gods of Babylon. We'll make ourselves Gods, images of metal or wood or stone.'

If you cannot worship the God who created you, then you worship a god that you yourself have created. And in our world, the most popular such God is money, and the things that money can buy. Time, that reminds us of our mortality, becomes an enemy, and we set up our Gods to defeat him, to blot him out, to pretend he isn't there. Our achievements, our possessions, our hectic so-called leisure, are all designed to hide from us the reality that time is ticking our life away.

To make a god of that which is not God is idolatry. And it doesn't work, because, as the prophets were not slow to point out, the idols have no life in them. Things have no power to renew our life. It is the Lord, who faints not neither is weary, who gives power to the faint—and to those who have no might, he increases strength.

How then do we live with cheerfulness and hope in this fleeting world? How do we live without anxiety in the face of an uncertain future, and without regret in the light of an unchangeable past?

First, when we set our faith, not in the work of our hands, but in the hands of God. We may see him, not only as the Saviour of our souls, but as the redeemer of our time, the renewer of our life. He takes our time seriously because he takes it up into his purposes, and makes of it something new—even those 'chronicles of wasted time' which seem to have been the story of our life:

*Even youths shall faint and be weary,*
*    and young men shall fall exhausted;*
*but they who wait for the Lord shall renew their strength,*
*    they shall mount up with wings like eagles,*
*they shall run and not be weary,*

*they shall walk and not faint.*

But, second, even in this human life we are already meeting, touching, those things that are eternal. You might say that what divides people from one another is the things that they value. Whether they value the things that pass, or the things that last. Recently I heard on the radio a silly discussion about the Seven Deadly Sins. What nobody suggested was that the so-called Deadly Sins are mostly about getting things out of proportion, putting an ultimate value on some thing, or aspect in life, which is good in itself, but becomes destructive when the possession of it becomes the be-all and end-all of existence: food, for example, or sex or money.

Paul speaks of the things that abide: faith and hope and love. He speaks elsewhere of the fruit of the spirit, which is love, joy, peace, patience, kindness, goodness, faithfulness, gentleness, self-control. He might have said of these also that these are things that abide. Treasures where thieves cannot break through or steal, which moth and rust cannot corrupt.

The greatest of these is love. Paul's song of love in 1 Corinthians may well be a pen-portrait of his master, Jesus Christ. Those who know that love in this life, know something that is not bounded by time, not limited by time, not frustrated by time—something that is the foretaste of eternity.

*Love's not Time's fool, though rosy lips and cheeks*
   *Within his bending sickle's compass come.*
*Love alters not with his brief hours and weeks,*
   *But bears it out even to the edge of doom.*
*If this be error and upon me proved,*
   *I never writ, nor no man ever loved.*

But for once in his life, Paul expressed it more eloquently even than Shakespeare when he said simply, 'Love never ends.'

Now to the God of Love, who, through Jesus Christ, has set his love in our hearts and given us the foretaste of the things that are eternal, to him be glory for ever and ever. Amen.

# 12

# The Candid Eye

ADMISSION OF FIRST COMMUNICANTS

*Readings:* Psalm 146; Luke 18:35 (to the end).

*Text:* Luke 18:41

> *Jesus said, 'What do you want me to do for you?' And he said,*
> *'Lord, that I may see again.'*

When I was a boy in Leith and Edinburgh, I used to see beggars
often. These were the years between the Wars. When I went up
town with my mother, we would see them in doorways, on
Princes Street and down Waverley Steps, in ragged clothes, with
a cloth cap laid out on the pavement, or holding out an enamel
mug—a tinny—for the coppers or threepenny bits which were
what people put in. Some of them wore medal ribbons, and had a
notice hanging round their neck which said 'Disabled Ex-Service-
man.'

You never knew, of course, who were genuinely in need and
who were frauds. Lots of stories used to go around, including the
one about the successful beggar whose chauffeur used to drop
him in the morning and pick him up at night! No one every
actually saw this happen—it was a myth—but the stories served
to justify our hard-heartedness and to ease our discomfort as we
passed these dregs of society on our way into Jenners.

Then, after the Second World War, there were many years
when we never saw a beggar on the streets, or hardly ever. Our

country in particular has sought to see that the victims of war should be helped and cared for, and that no one should be left in want or homeless or destitute.

It seems to be an achievement—a very doubtful achievement —of our modern self-help society that the beggars are back on our pavements again.

In the east, of course, they are always there, and in the cities of India the pavement is home to many. Some of them are disabled —the lame or the limbless or the blind. In many countries still, if you are disabled or blind, you cannot work, and there is no way you can eat unless you beg. So, in Jesus' day, the beggar was a common sight, and for the blind in particular, begging was often the only means of survival. So, in the urban landscape of Palestine in the first century the beggar was a common feature, and there are other references to beggars in the New Testament—in the parables of Jesus, in the Gospel story and in Acts.

The story we read is a story of a man who has been reduced by blindness to begging for his bread. Jesus and the twelve are on the way up to Jerusalem for the Passover feast. They fall in, it seems, with a larger band of pilgrims also from Galilee who are on their way to Jerusalem. It was safer to travel in a largish group.

The crowd was making a lot of noise, some of them maybe singing Psalms, and others talking about this Jesus who had joined them. He was a celebrity. Many of them would have heard him preach and seen him heal, and were in their own way followers, wondering if he was the leader they were looking for who would set their country free.

Anyway, this blind man was sitting by the roadside begging— perhaps just outside the city gates of Jericho. He hears the noisy crowd and asks what all the commotion is about. The answer is not 'There's a band of pilgrims going up to Jerusalem', but 'Jesus of Nazareth is passing by.' That's why there's the noise, that's why there's the buzz of excitement. It's because Jesus is passing. Immediately the blind man begins to shout out, above the noise, 'Jesus, Son of David, pity me.'

The word which Luke uses is one of the few Greek words which came to be used in the worship of the Church through the centuries, in the Latin mass as well as in the Eastern rites. Those of you who are music lovers will know it—*Kyrie eleison*, 'Lord, have mercy.' That's the word the blind man uses, when he shouts above the throng. 'Jesus, Son of David, have mercy on me.'

His friends try to shut him up. Now why should they do that? He wasn't doing any harm, shouting at Jesus whom he couldn't see. I can't think why, unless it was the title he used to address Jesus—'Son of David'. That was one of the titles of the Messiah, the leader who was to come to deliver them and restore their country's freedom. By calling Jesus 'Son of David', the blind man shows that he believes all the talk he has heard about Jesus, that he is the expected one, the Son of David. But that was dangerous talk, seditious talk. If he goes shouting that in the street, he might get himself into trouble, he might get *them* into trouble, he might get *Jesus* into trouble. So it's, 'Shut up, don't talk like that.' But he goes on, shouting all the more, 'Son of David, pity me!'

Jesus stops and asks to see him, and the man is led through the throng to the one who is at the heart of it all. He hears a voice of kindness saying, 'What do you want me to do for you?' The answer is immediate. It's not for alms he has been shouting, not for another copper in his tinny. 'Lord, that I may see again.' The word suggests that he has known what it is to see. He has lost his sight and he wants it back, for to him sight is life, it's independence, it's freedom from the humiliation of begging. Then the voice says with authority, 'Have your sight back. It is your faith that has made you well.' And the story ends with him following Jesus, glorifying God, and all the people praising God.

Some of you may be like me, a little uncomfortable with the miracle stories in the Gospels. St Luke loves them. He was a doctor, and he liked to show Jesus as a healer. I don't doubt that Jesus was a healer, though he himself had a way of telling his patients, as he did with this blind man, that they had healed themselves. 'Your faith has saved you.'

My problem with healing miracles is not that I don't understand how they happened. There are plenty of things in life that I don't understand—more as I get older. My problem is always with the people who don't get healed. In Jesus' day in Palestine there were lots of sick people who weren't restored to health, lots of lame who didn't leap, lots of haemorrhages that were not staunched. There were many blind beggars by other roadsides who didn't hear Jesus of Nazareth passing by.

Our doctors can do so much that Luke the beloved physician could never do. If you develop cataract, you may hope at some point to go into hospital and have your sight restored. A detached retina they can now treat with care. But there are other conditions for which they can do very little. It is still the case that some are healed and some not.

We pray for healing. I hope all of us do when someone we know is sick. Sometimes our prayers are answered, and we are quietly grateful. But often they are not—not in that way anyway. Is it our lack of faith? I hope not. It seems that God has different ways with different people. Some have health restored. Some show his strength through their weakness, and find new ways to serve because they have been laid aside. Some go on ahead to remind us that it is through death that we come to eternal life. There are different ways of following Jesus.

This man used his new-found wholeness to glorify God and to follow Jesus on the road to Jerusalem. What happened to him afterwards, I wonder? Mark gives us his name—Bartimaeus—

which suggests that he might have been known in the early Church, as a member of it. Matthew typically has two blind men —he likes pairs. But where Luke differs from the others is where he puts this story. The others put it at the end of the journey— the last event before the Palm Sunday procession into Jerusalem. Luke puts it at the beginning. He changes Mark's order. Clearly he has a reason for doing this, and the reason is in verses 31-35. Jesus said to the twelve, 'Behold we go up to Jerusalem'—and he foretold his arrest, his humiliation his death and his rising. 'But,' says Luke, 'they understood none of these things. This saying was hid from them, and they did not grasp what was said.' Three times he tells us that they didn't understand. They were blind. They couldn't see.

Does Luke put the two stories together to suggest that it was easier for Jesus to give the beggar back his sight than to cure the blindness of the twelve? Or is he telling us that we are all blind, until we ask Jesus to make us see?

There are young people here today who have come to a turning-point, a staging post, a Jericho perhaps, in their pilgrimage, as they come to profess their faith and take the vows of communicant membership. For some perhaps this is a very natural stage in the road they have been travelling, following Jesus. For others, maybe, the time of preparation for first communion has been an opening of the eyes, and you have begun to see things in Christianity, in Jesus, that you never saw before.

Whichever it is, you are possibly all aware that there are a lot of things that you don't see clearly yet, or don't see at all. It's not any easier for us than it was for the twelve to see what Jesus was saying to them, which is that life is gained through death, that triumph comes through suffering. We see some things only in glimpses.

There is one gift I would pray to God for you, the first communicants today, and that is that you may have the candid eye. The gift of the candid eye, the courage to see things as they really are, and to call them by their proper names.

The clear vision not to be taken in by the claptrap—the religious claptrap and the political claptrap and the commercial claptrap that is all around us today. It's an uncomfortable gift, the candid eye, for it strips us of all our comfortable prejudices, it robs us of the cliches and the slogans and the shibboleths that save us from thinking and from seeing. But it is the gift of life itself, because without the honest and the candid eye we never experience life as it really is.

So perhaps the blind man's request should be the prayer of all of us today. Jesus says to us, 'What do you want me to do for you?' We answer, 'Lord, that I may see.' Then, seeing, we will follow.

# 13

# Taking the Cross

*Reading:* Mark 8:31-38

*Text:* Mark 8:34

> *And he called to him the multitude with his disciples, and said to them, 'If any man would come after me, let him deny himself and take up his cross and follow me.'*

This has been called one of the 'hard sayings' of Jesus. These hard sayings seem to me to be hard in two senses. The first sense is 'hard to understand'—the question we're left with is, 'What exactly does Jesus mean when he says that?' The second sense is 'hard to take'—'He can't really mean that we do that, surely?' The texts tend to be those which make a difficult demand.

This text seems to be of the second kind of hardness—a difficult demand. 'If anyone will come after me, let him deny himself and take up his cross and follow me.' That's not an easy or an inviting prospect. But as we'll see, the text is hard in the other sense also, because it's not easy to see precisely what denying yourself or taking up your cross or following Jesus means in our day and generation.

Our age doesn't take kindly to talk about self-denial or taking up the cross. We are fed on advertisements which promise us instant satisfactions. If our shoes start to hurt we throw them away and buy another pair. If marriage begins to hurt and fails to satisfy, we start thinking straight away about divorce. It would seem that our generation is not deeply into self-denial or bearing the cross. And we don't talk in these terms very much.

It was different with the Victorians. They used these terms freely.

When I began to think about this text, the first thing that came into my mind was a verse from a children's hymn, which some of you may know.

*There's not a child so small and weak*
*But has his little cross to take.*

That comes from the last verse of the hymn 'We are but little children weak, nor born in any high estate.' It was written, somewhere before 1850, by Cecil Frances Alexander, the wife of an Anglican clergyman in Ireland. She was the author of 'There is a green hill far away'—a fine hymn—but 'We are but little children weak' is hardly her finest effort. As she herself explained, 'It was written for very poor children in a crowded city Sunday School.' Perhaps the little cross they had to take was having to go to Sunday School and sing dreadful hymns like that.

The reason why I'm talking about the hymn is that it illustrates one way of understanding—or is it *mis*-understanding?—the call to take up your cross.

The Victorian Sunday School for very poor children taught them that their poverty was a cross laid on them by God, and that they must be mild and contented under it. It was nice and easy for the rich and comfortable to preach such lessons to the children of the poor. But it was a cop-out: using religion to justify the injustices of the social order. 'The opium of the people' was what Karl Marx called it.

Now even in our high-tech age, there are many circumstances

in life which we can do nothing about and which we just have to bear. There are illnesses which medical science can't yet cure or relieve. Some of these are very painful and some very disabling. It's a humbling and a heartening experience to watch someone coping with disability and with pain and coming out triumphant. Is that cross-bearing? We often talk of the chronic sick or the disabled as having a cross to bear. But is that it?

I may be wrong, but I think that the important thing is how the disability or difficulty is accepted. If it is carried with dignity and even triumph, we recognise that here is a burden which has become a cross. If it is taken with complaint and resentment, it remains simply a burden.

If it is taken with complaint and resentment then, of course, it is the other people who have a cross to bear—that of caring for a difficult and complaining person. Perhaps they also have a choice as to whether it is simply a burden or becomes a cross.

Now in our age, even within our own highly-developed society, there are also many poor and many homeless—indeed, their number is increasing. Perhaps poverty can also be a burden or a cross. But it ill behoves any of us to say so, because poverty is not inevitable, homelessness is not necessary. It is because the rest of us don't care enough. I do not think I can tell someone that their arthritic hip is a cross they have to bear if they are waiting years in pain while someone with a less serious condition can jump every queue because they have money or private insurance or a GP who is managing his own budget. That is not a cross, it is a scandal. And it is the same with poverty. I'm chary of the rich preaching contentment to the poor.

There is something about 'taking a cross' which is different from 'having a cross to bear.' The first is a voluntary act. It is something you do, you accept, not just something you put up with. I suggested that that may be the difference between a burden and a cross. The burden that is accepted and carried without resentment becomes a cross.

This leads me to a further thought. Perhaps a difference between a burden and a cross is that the cross is carried out of love: love for God or love for others. The particular person I had in mind when I spoke about coping with disability and pain was someone who was uncomplaining and in a strange way triumphant because she was always interested in other people, concerned about others, never wrapped up in self. Everyone who loves carries a cross, everyone who cares is a cross-bearer. The more you care, the more you feel for the sin and the pain of humanity. The more you are committed to help and to serve, the more you are going to find a cross on your back.

Luke inserts the word 'daily' into our text. We must take up our cross daily. Cross-taking is not an extraordinary thing. It is part of the daily business of Christian living and loving. So it was with Jesus.

But because it is his cross that we take up when we love, we find that that cross is carrying us, and blessing and sustaining us.

Now does that give us a clue about self-denial? The demand that we deny ourselves, literally say 'No' to self, has sometimes been interpreted in very extreme forms. The ascetics believed that they should deny themselves everything that they could possibly do without. St Jerome, who gloried in every form of self-denial, and encouraged others to it also, believed that it was a luxury to eat food cooked if it could possibly be eaten raw; and a luxury to eat at all if it was possible to do without. And of course, any form of sexual activity was looked upon as self-indulgence.

It is clear that if you go along that line, there is no end to self-denial, short of suicide. You deny yourself, until you kill yourself. (Astonishingly the early ascetics lived often to a great age—though what fun they got out of that I've never discovered.)

Such self-denial is in fact self-centred. The self-denial which is a forgetfulness of self is quite different. Calvin understood the Christian life in terms of self-denial, but for Calvin this was never the self-centredness of the ascetic, but the self-forgetfulness of those whose life is lived in gratitude to God and in love for their neighbour.

So self-denial is an aspect of love. Of course, people do deny themselves for a host of reasons—a great deal of self-denial is practised today by people who go on slimming diets. Sometimes that is for the sake of their health. Sometimes it is in search of the perfect form, sometimes a longing for lost youth. Many of these motives are quite self-centred, but some are for the sake of others, for the sake of the family, or in order to be a fitter and better servant of God.

But for most of us, the occasions of self-denial are not things we have to look for, or impose artificially on ourselves, like giving up things for Lent. The occasions of self-denial come with the morning post, with the chance conversation in the street, with the telephone call which tells us that someone is ill and needing help. The loving person possibly has no thought of self-denial when personal plans are shelved, and action is taken to help in someone else's emergency. Self-denial it is, though its other name is love.

And this is what it is to follow Jesus, for he himself is the great example of what it is to be available for others in love.

Mark says that he called the multitude. So this hard saying is not just for the close group of the twelve, it is for everyone who can hear. For to deny yourself and take up our cross and follow Jesus is the way of love which is the way of life for every one of us.

# 14

# Easter Fear

*Readings:* Romans 6:1-4; 8:9-11; Mark 16:1-8

*Text:* Mark 16:8

*And they said nothing to anyone, for they were afraid.*

Most novels, plays, sermons even, end with a punch-line in which the author rounds it off, and the reader, the theatre audience, or the congregation, feel satisfied that things are complete, nothing more needs to be said. Thinking of this I picked at random a novel from my shelves—it was Iris Murdoch's *The Sandcastle*. Her last sentences are, 'Everything was all right now. It was all right. It was all right.' I think you'll agree that you can hardly have a more satisfactory sentiment than that on which to end a novel—everything all right.

But when Mark ends his Gospel, it is not with the complacency and satisfaction of Iris Murdoch, or the roundedness of most sermons. His story ends with bewilderment and fear.

'And they said nothing to anyone, for they were afraid.'

What a strange way to end the greatest story ever told. Because this, I have little doubt, is how Mark did end it. It is just possible that the last page of the Gospel got torn off, but that isn't likely. What we do know is that is seemed so unsatisfactory to the early readers of the Gospel, that different attempts were made to finish it off. One of these is given in our Bible as verses 9-20 of chapter

16, but it clearly is not by Mark but has been cobbled together out of different things in the other Gospels and Acts. There is a shorter ending, which is given as a footnote in the Revised Standard Version, but that is possibly an even later attempt to round the book off.

Can it be that Mark ended his Gospel without a single story of a resurrection appearance of Jesus to his disciples? It seems that he may have had in mind to tell some of these stories, because the mysterious young man whom the women find sitting in the tomb says, 'But go, tell his disciples and Peter that he is going before you to Galilee; there you will see him, as he told you.' There is that hint that something more is to happen and it is to happen in Galilee, up in the north in their home country. But meantime the book ends, and it ends with the picture of bewildered women leaving the tomb, dumfoonert, and afraid.

'And they said nothing to anyone.' The Greek is literally 'they said nothing to nobody.' You can say that in Scots. William Lorimer in his *New Testament in Scots* translates it, 'An they tauld naebodie naething', which is good Scots. But it would be bad English to say, 'They told nobody nothing. For they were afraid.'

I find these simple words among the most authentic in the New Testament. They have the right feel about them—for there is something quite unchancy about all of this, something unnerving. For the human being, nothing is so certain as death, nothing is so final as burial. To those who die, we say the last goodbye. We may travel a long way to be at a funeral, because it is important for us to say goodbye to an old friend.

So it was for these women. The last thing they could do for this glorious young man, this beloved master, was to bring the spices to give his crucified body the ritual anointing which had been omitted in the haste to bury him before the Sabbath. It is an odd thing that in male-dominated societies the men do the killing and then leave it to the women to clear up the mess that they have made—women prepare the corpses for burial. It happens still in Ireland, and one feels that if only the men had to face the horror of what they had done, there might be less enthusiasm for the armalite and the bomb.

The women are on their way before they think about the difficulty that awaits them. A great boulder had been rolled up to seal the mouth of the rock-tomb. How were they to get in, and no one about at that hour in the morning? Why had they not thought of that before they started? The next thing they saw, the mouth of the cave was open, the stone rolled back. Someone must have been up before them. Inside, not a dead body, but this mysterious young man. Who was he and where had he come from? How did he know all that he was telling them? The world has suddenly turned upside down. Are they awake or are they dreaming? What is delusion and what reality? The one human instinct that still seems to work is the instinct that tells their feet to run, and run they do. 'And they went out and fled from the tomb, for trembling and astonishment had come upon them; and they said nothing to anyone, for they were afraid.'

I wonder if the authentic Easter experience is not just that— the experience of bewildered surprise, dumfoonert and feart. That is the start of it anyway, and maybe until we have been there with the women, the other Easter experiences can't really be ours. Oh, I love the stories in the other Gospels: John's tender account of the encounter of Jesus with Mary Magdalene at the tomb, Luke's story of the mysterious traveller on the Emmaus road. I identify strongly with Thomas in the upper room. But I come back to these women and their breathless fear, because for them the boundaries of life and death are not so neat and tidy as they had supposed, and there is something uncanny going on here.

Matthew took Mark's story as the basis of his account: but

whereas for Mark the picture is in black-and-white, with the early morning mists swirling around, making everything unreal, Matthew gives it to us in glorious technicolour. There is a touch of the Cecil B de Mille about Matthew. First there is a great earthquake; then the mysterious young man of Mark has, in Matthew, become an unmistakable angel who rolls the stone away in front of the women, then sits on it and talks to them. They take all this remarkably calmly, and then depart, not in flight but in haste, and their feeling is not just fear, but great joy. The tone of Matthew is different, and, I must admit, I prefer Mark. There must be something about the resurrection that takes our breath away, that leaves us wondering and more than a little afraid.

People who have done research into religious experiences have found that more people than one might think have had experiences that you would call religious: but most of them have never spoken about them to anyone. 'And they said nothing to anyone, for they were afraid.' That experience of the women is repeated in the more trivial, though sometimes not so trivial, experiences of ordinary people today. The things that make you wonder, that take your breath away, are not easy to talk about and are not lightly shared. Now it is good when people can be encouraged to share their experiences—as has happened in some of our Easter services—and we are all encouraged thereby. But I think we all have more respect for a religion that is somewhat reticent, rather than for one that is glib.

'Were you there when they rolled away the stone?' asks the negro spiritual. Now the answer, quite literally, is that we were not. Indeed, was anyone? We don't know. What I do know is that Easter faith is not a glib belief in something that happened in the past. Nor is it simply the celebration of the returning spring, the expected cycle of new life and new blossom. Easter is about the utterly unexpected, a breaking-in, an interruption of our ordinary experience. It is something that causes you to tremble, tremble, tremble, because you realise that if Christ is risen, then the world is being turned upside down.

My dear wife often said that if anyone would understand the Easter faith, they must sing the Easter hymns. I think that is true, for it is in poetry and in music that this bewilderment, this surprise, this wonder, can be expressed. The speech of the heart, not just of the head. But perhaps the sacraments also express it, in ways that go beyond ordinary speech, and hold out before us the surprising possibilities of new life in Christ. Do we not catch our breath at the baptism of a child?

Paul says:

*Do you not know that all of us who have been baptised into Christ Jesus were baptised into his death? We were buried therefore with him by baptism into death, so that as Christ was raised from the dead by the glory of the Father, we too might walk in newness of life.*

Does that thought not take your breath away? Sometimes it causes me to tremble, tremble, tremble. What possibilities there are now! In what surprising ways and places the risen Christ may yet meet you and me, calling us to newness of life! Life is literally open-ended. No wonder the women ran away, and said nothing to no one. They were afraid.

# 15

# Compelling Evidence

*Readings:* Job 14:1-12; John 20:19-31

*Text:* John 20:25

> *So the other disciples told him, 'We have seen the Lord.' But he said to them, 'Unless I see in his hands the print of the nails, and place my finger in the mark of the nails and place my hand in his side, I will not believe.'*

Unless I see in his hands the print of the nails, and place my finger in the mark of the nails and place my hand in his side, I will not believe.

I've been thinking a bit about evidence recently. What constitutes evidence? What makes something evident? A thing is evident when it is clearly visible. Philosophers used to think that certain truths were self-evident—you just had to say them to know they were true. That good is better than evil would be an example. But where something isn't obvious or visible—*eg* who committed the murder on the Orient Express—then you need evidence to point to the murderer. On the other hand, we know that our eyes can often be deceived, and that we jump to conclusions that aren't justified. In real life we don't always have Hercule Poirot to sort it all out and bring it to a satisfactory conclusion.

No. In real life we have the Birmingham Six, committed to prison for the Birmingham pub bombings, found guilty on the evidence of the police and forensic experts, on evidence which seemed unassailable. Only recently has it been established that the police evidence was fabricated and the forensic evidence unreliable. It took many years and a considerable number of determined doubting Thomases, who questioned the evidence and looked for more reliable evidence, before these judgments could be overturned.

When stories of ritual abuse are not taken seriously, children may suffer. But when they are too readily believed, innocent families, parents and children, may suffer an appalling kind of abuse for which there is no apparent redress. Do we not need some doubting Thomases to insist on the evidence that will protect the innocent?

Now terrible things do happen, and often we're unwilling to admit that our nice civilised world contains such cruelty, such cold calculated horror. It isn't so easy to avoid it, however, nowadays. We see it on our TV and in our newspapers. On the international scale, genocide and starvation; and, on the level of the family, the abuse of children by their parents.

Of course, the stories we read and hear are not always true. Some of the horror stories are disinformation put about by governments for propaganda and political purposes. The Americans are good at this, and our government is not far behind.

I've a great respect for Amnesty International, who have done so much for the release of political prisoners, and against torture and oppression. I respect them because they are politically evenhanded, between Left and Right, and because they never publish a story until they have verified it as far as is humanly possible. They respect the evidence.

But most of us readily believe the propaganda stories, because they fit in with our prejudices. We are all good at seeing the evidence that supports our prejudices and ignoring whatever challenges them. We don't like changing our minds or admitting that we've made a mistake. When we have a cause that amounts to an obsession, then we interpret everything in terms of our obsession. The contrary evidence is brushed aside.

Respect for the evidence is respect for truth. Thomas doesn't want to believe something that isn't true. That is even more so because it is not a terrible thing, but a wonderful thing, that he is being asked to believe. 'We have seen the Lord.' Thomas refuses to be guilty of wishful thinking.

I have a running argument with some of my friends who keep talking, and writing too, about our society as a secular society: a society without religious beliefs. I tell them that that is wishful thinking on their part, because they like to think of the Church as a small minority in a pagan world. But the evidence seems to me to suggest that ours is a persistently and stubbornly religious society, even a superstitious society. People will believe almost anything that anybody, puffed by good publicity, tells them.

I remember in my first charge, I had a Sunday evening discussion group which consisted mostly of young or youngish adults, and it was very refreshing, because they loved to get their teeth into things, and we had revealing and helpful discussions about worship, the sacraments, belief. We had been talking about how little people knew their Bible, so they asked me, the next Sunday, to give them a Bible quiz. So I did. We divided them into teams, and the group which was captained by my organist was doing very badly—until I asked them the question, 'Who swallowed the whale?' All fingers on the buzzer, or rather hands up, and from my organist I got the answer, 'Jonah.' I looked at my friend sadly and seriously and said, 'Some people will swallow anything.'

But I have heard someone say that if he read in the Bible that Jonah had swallowed the whale, he would believe it. I cannot myself think that that kind of credulity is the highest kind of faith. Faith is not about how much you can swallow. Faith is a view of things, of what matters in this life of ours. Faith is something by which you live, and it is always being tested by life itself, the things we do and the things that happen to us.

That's why we need people like Job, who won't accept the slick theology of his friends who say, 'Bad things happen to bad people. If you suffer, you must have done wrong.' Job won't have that. That's not the way the world is, and Job is prepared to stand up to God and say so.

That's why we need people like Thomas, determined not to be too easily persuaded. The only faith that is worth having today is a critical faith, a faith prepared to be challenged, questioned, that faces honestly the difficulties life places in its way, that weighs the evidence. A strong faith needs to be seasoned with scepticism.

Unless I see in his hands the print of the nails, and place my finger in the mark of the nails and place my hand in his side, I will not believe.

Now it must be obvious to you that by talking in praise of Thomas, I'm saying something different from what the New Testament seems to say. I can imagine some of you wriggling inwardly, as I often do when hearing sermons, and saying to yourselves, 'But that's not the point.' Thomas is not often praised for his sceptical attitude. In sermons we are usually told not to be 'doubting Thomases.' That seems to be the attitude of John and of Jesus in the Gospel. 'Have you believed because you have seen me? Blessed are those who have not seen and yet believe.'

It's true, as John well knew, that Thomas was in a privileged position. The kind of evidence he was insisting on, seeing and touching the scars of Jesus, is a luxury which is not available to us. What kind of evidence do we then have that compels us to believe that Jesus is alive and risen from the dead?

There are different answers to that question. One is to say that we don't need evidence, for we believe it on authority—the authority of the Church or of the Church and the Bible together, in the case of Roman Catholics; the authority of the Bible alone, in the case of Protestants. The Church teaches ... or the Bible says ... and that's enough. You must not question what the Church teaches or the Bible says. That's one view, the view of Christian conservatism, whether Catholic or Protestant.

A variant on that is to say you simply believe. You either have faith or you don't have faith, that's all it is. Evidence doesn't enter into it. It isn't necessary. Faith is its own evidence.

Now all these things, it seems to me, have truth in them. I pay attention to the Church's tradition, though I recognise that the Church and the Churches have taught many different things through the centuries and they can't all be true. And I go to the Bible as the source-book of Christian faith, but the Bible contains many different points of view, and it's a struggle to find what the Bible is really saying.

Nor do I think that faith is just the conclusion of an argument, like a summing up of the evidence to enable the jury to come to its verdict, guilty, not-guilty, or not proven: risen, not risen, or don't know. Faith is personal conviction. It's something you stake your life on.

But what worries me about the kinds of religion I've just mentioned—the religions of external authority or of internal experience—is that they leave religion up in the air, a religious world which never touches the ground of the public world of our buying and selling and earning our daily bread. I can know that my religion is reality and not fantasy only if it makes sense of that public world and my life within it.

That is the kind of evidence Job was looking for as he looked bleakly at the world as it was without finding evidence for resurrection. That is the kind of evidence Thomas was looking for as he refused to believe until the evidence compelled him. That is the kind of evidence we need.

And that is the kind of religion we can commend to others. I cannot commend a religion based on authority, because such religion is always oppressive. I cannot commend a religion based only on inner experience, because such experience is essentially private.

Thomas, keeping his feet well on the ground, asked for the kind of evidence that made sense to him. I also need some evidence. I believe in the Resurrection not just because of what others have told me (though I respect what they have told me) nor just because I wish to believe it (though I do), but because my life and my world make sense if Jesus is alive, and they make no sense at all if he has simply been dead these two thousand years.

That faith is constantly under challenge from the evil, the pain, the suffering of the world. How can there be a loving God in a world such as this? But when we face the evil, the pain, the suffering squarely, we find there is only one story we can tell to it, only one story that illuminates it, and that is the Cross and Resurrection of Jesus Christ.

When our feet are firmly on the ground of the world's sad and terrible realities, we find to our surprise that we are face to face with the living Christ, and there is wrung from our lips the cry of faith, 'My Lord and my God.'

# 16

# Comfort in our Tears

MEMORIAL SERVICE FOR VICTIMS
OF THE AIR DISASTER AT LOCKERBIE (4 JANUARY 1989)

*Readings:* 2 Corinthians 1:2-7; John 11:17-27

*Text:* 2 Corinthians 1:7

> *Our hope for you is unshaken; for we know that as you share
> in our sufferings, you will also share in our comfort.*

When Martha greeted Jesus after the death of her brother Lazarus,
it was with a word of reproach, even though deep within that
reproach there was a pained and protesting faith. 'Lord, if you
had been here, my brother would not have died.'

In every untimely bereavement, whether it is the quiet slip-
ping from life of one most dearly loved, or whether it is awful
disaster striking hundreds in the sky and from the sky, our first
act of pained, protesting faith is to turn to God in reproach, even
in anger. 'Lord, if you had been here, my brother—my sister, my
beloved, my child—would not have died.' Why did this happen
to him, to her, to me? Why was disaster not averted by the touch
of an almighty hand? Martha speaks for us all. 'Lord, if you had
been here .... '

Where has he been then, when all this happened? Absent?
Looking the other way? The Christian answer to the age-old
question why a good God permits evil is a strange one, because the
Christian faith is that God is there where we might least expect to

find him—in the disaster, in the tragedy, in the suffering. From Christmas to Easter, from Bethlehem to Calvary and the Emmaus Road—that is the message of Christian faith. He is not outside it all, absent, indifferent, untouched. He is in it. When Jesus hung upon the cross, Martha could not reproach him then, 'Lord, if you had been here, my Master would not have died.' In that dying, Jesus set the seal upon his sharing with us in all our human life, our human suffering and loss.

When we cry in our pain, we cry to the one who knows pain, who shares it with us. That is strange comfort, and it does not take away our pain, but may give it meaning, as with a flash of light. When Paul speaks of God's comfort to those who are in trouble, he goes on immediately to talk about the sufferings of Christ—our sharing of his sufferings and his sharing of ours, for it is in the fellowship of suffering that we will find our God and know his comfort. If we could avoid the pain of being human, the pain of loving and losing, the pain of suffering with those who suffer, we would be choosing to stand aloof from humanity and apart from God.

'And our hope for you is well-grounded,' said Paul, 'for we know that if you have part in the suffering, you have part also in the divine consolation.'

But it is not only pain and grief that we feel at this catastrophe, it is also indignation. For this was not an unforeseeable natural disaster, such as earthquake. Nor was it the result of human error or carelessness. This, we now know, was an act of human wickedness. That such carnage of the young and of the innocent should have been willed by men in cold and calculated evil, is horror upon horror.

What is our response to that?

The desire, the determination, that those who did this should be detected and, if possible, brought to justice, is natural and is right. The uncovering of the truth will not be easy, and evidence that would stand up in a court of law may be hard to obtain.

Justice is one thing. But already one hears in the media the word 'retaliation'. As far as I know, no responsible politician has used that word, and I hope none ever will, except to disown it. For that way lies the endless cycle of violence upon violence, horror upon horror. And we may be tempted, indeed urged by some, to flex our muscles in response, to show that we are men. To show that we are *what*? To show that we are prepared to let more young and more innocent die, to let more rescue workers labour in more wreckage to find the grisly proof, not of our virility, but of our inhumanity. That is what retaliation means. I, for one, will have none of it, and I hope you will not either.

Justice yes, retaliation no. For if we move in the way of retaliation we move right outside of the fellowship of Christ's sufferings, outside of the divine consolation. There is nothing that way but bitterness, and the destruction of our own humanity.

Atrocities, acts of cold and calculated evil, on the individual level and on the mass scale, are not something novel on the human scene. To be sure, modern science has made available weapons and explosives that Genghis Khan could not have dreamed about. But evil and destructiveness are not new. The crucifixion of Jesus was an act of cold and calculated evil, involving the subversion of the justice for which the Roman state was renowned. Christ's sufferings are the sufferings of the innocent at the hands of evil and unscrupulous men, and it is these we share when we suffer at the hands of the evil and the unscrupulous in our time. So if he is not here in Lockerbie, he is not anywhere.

But there has been not only suffering here, there has been courage and sacrifice and understanding and compassion. A whole community reaching out with open hearts and open homes and willing hands to sustain and comfort those who have suffered loss. Rescue workers, soldiers, RAF, police and civilians ready to work their hearts out to see what can be recovered from the wreckage. A co-ordination of essential services and of pastoral care so that those whose lives and homes have been shattered here, and those who have made the long sad journey across the Atlantic, may be met with sensitive understanding and generous support and care.

Where was God in all of that? Can anyone doubt that he was right there in the midst of it? If here in the midst of evil we find goodness, if here in the midst of darkness we find light, if here in the midst of desolation we find ourselves strangely comforted, can we doubt that our lives are touched by the God of all comfort, the God whose consolation never fails?

It is the experience of humankind, that when we walk through the valley of the shadow, we are not helped by smooth words spoken from a safe distance, but by those who have known the darkness and are prepared to share it with us, and hold us till we see the light. That is the way the comfort of God touches us and holds us. For it is as we share the suffering that we share the comfort. 'Our hope for you is unshaken,' says Paul, 'for we know that if you share in our sufferings, you will also share in our comfort.'

Now, blessed be the God and Father of our Lord Jesus Christ, the Father of mercies and God of all comfort, who comforts us in all our afflictions, so that we may be able to comfort those who are in any affliction, with the comfort with which we ourselves are comforted by God, to whom be glory for ever.